A Special Gift

To _____

From _____

& Other Touches
from an Everyday God

Carol Greenwood

Fairmont Books is a ministry of The McDougal Foundation, Inc., a Maryland nonprofit corporation dedicated to spreading the Gospel of the Lord Jesus Christ to as many people as possible in the shortest time possible.

Published by:

𝒻airmont Books
P.O. Box 3595
Hagerstown, MD 21742-3595
www.mcdougalpublishing.com

ISBN 1-58158-049-5
(Formerly ISBN 0-932305-87-3)

Printed in the United States of America
For Worldwide Distribution

Dedication

To my husband and best friend, Dick. And, to our growing family—Anne, Alan, Andrea and Olivia; Gail, Dan and Rachel; Paul, Ginny, Chelsea, David and Kate; Jane, Shane, Hannah, Thomas and Sarah.

I'm so glad we could live many of these stories together.

Acknowledgements

My profound thanks go to my family for their love, their support, their critiques and their willingness to be shown as human in our family stories. Special thanks to daughter Gail, whose typing and expert editorial skills were a vital contribution to this book.

Contents

CHAPTER ELEVEN

CHAPTER TWELVE

Foreword

Dirty dishes. Runny noses. Spilled milk. Scattered news-papers. Friends who forget our birthdays. Children who quarrel. Deaths of loved ones. The tattered fabric of an every-day life. It's tedium *ad nauseam* unless you are looking for something else.

But for those who are, like our creative author Carol Green-wood, the garment of life is filled with pockets of joy, moments of wonder, soarings of inspiration and insights into God in the most everyday moments.

God didn't come to be shut up in a cathedral. He came to be like us: to walk in sorrow and joy, pain and peace, weari-ness and exuberance—just like you and I do every day. He came to understand us, and because He does, He is found in the most mundane warp and woof of life. So put your hand deep in the folds of life to find the treasures hidden there.

Reading this book will awaken you to the nearness of a Father God who understands. Who cares. Who encourages His tired, discouraged children. You will come away from this book knowing, in a fresh new way, God's unconditional love for each of us.

You will want to share this book with all those you love, because you will want them, too, to experience a newness of understanding of the God who walks beside us every day.

Joyful reading to you!

Gwen Ellis

Preface

"I had always felt life first as a story: and if there is a story, there is a story-teller."

G.K. Chesterton
Orthodoxy

"Where does God live?" Our granddaughter Hannah needed an answer—now. Never mind that her mother, on countdown before guests arrived, was on her knees scrubbing the kitchen floor, rising up every few minutes to check on the roast in the oven.

But a five-year-old with a pressing theological question couldn't wait for a more convenient time. She persisted: "Mommy, where does God live? In Heaven?"

"Yeah, sure," Mommy said. "Daddy and I'll explain more at bedtime."

For fifteen silent minutes, Hannah pondered the answer. Then, she popped back into the kitchen to talk about "God's address" one more time. "Mommy, it seems strange to me that a God who loves us so much would live so far away."

Hannah's own heart nailed the truth: Our God is not a far-away God. Is it any wonder Jesus had such endearing words for little children? Kids like Hannah, who unashamedly spill out what their hearts really yearn for. In Hannah's case, she wanted to know how close our God really comes. That's an important question—even for adults. Do we serve a God who enters into our everyday lives? If so, how do we know His presence?

The adults Jesus talked with wanted an answer to these questions too. To help them know God, Jesus told simple

11

stories illustrating His Father's heart—His passion to love, to forgive, to comfort, to heal, to teach and to encourage. Jesus' stories about everyday life caught the attention of His hearers, then unfolded—and kept unfolding—with truth that had the power to change their hearts and their lives.

There's something about a story that, like my writer friend, Deena, says, "invites you in." As a story-lover, I've found that to be true. Time and time again, I've been drawn in to laughter and a fresh perspective, insight and hope as I've stepped back from the mundane and hectic for a moment or two, breathed in deeply and leaned into the pure delight of hearing someone's story. Perhaps you can recall those stories that made a difference in your life. Stories told and retold around your family table. Maybe even one a stranger shared with you on a plane flight or one a colleague told you over coffee break.

When I listen to someone's story, I am, for a few uninterrupted moments, a contented guest, invited into another place and another's life. I have never left those times without being enriched by the story—and the storyteller.

A Rose for Nana is a collection of stories about real people living ordinary lives. People like you and me who are continually surprised by a gracious God moving in close to find us right where we live. A God who is not put off by our lostness, but rather pursues us with His lavish, rescuing love. A God who even dares to call us His friends as we choose to pass on His love to others.

Most of the stories in *A Rose for Nana* first appeared as columns in "The Encourager," a regular feature of *Aglow* magazine. In this book's second printing, additional stories have been included. Be encouraged as you encounter Jesus within these pages. May you experience Him as the One who brings love down to find you—and to bring you hope.

Carol Greenwood
Seattle, Washington

CHAPTER ONE

A
Touch
of
Forgiveness

Jesus said, "Father, forgive them, for they do not know what they are doing."

Luke 23:34

A Rose for Nana

*B*uy *her flowers—today.* The nudge hit me five paces past the flower shop.

Great idea. I'll dash in on my way back from the park, I told myself, wanting to maintain stride and not lose the aerobic benefits of my walk. *I'll bring Nana a fresh rosebud with some baby's breath.*

Nana, as we called my eighty-one-year-old mother-in-law, loved flowers. And before Dad died and she moved to an apartment, she gardened like crazy. In recent years, however, her innate Scandinavian thrift joined forces with her Depression mentality and she rarely allowed herself the luxury of fresh cut flowers. In fact, whenever we crossed the state to visit her, she invariably reminded us not to bring her anything—especially flowers.

"They cost too much, and they just die anyway. Besides," she explained, "you and Dick need the money for the kids' education."

Eventually, I stopped arguing and resigned myself to arriving empty-handed at her doorstep.

But the issue with Nana went deeper than "no flowers, please." I'd struggled with her bluntness for years, ever since Dick and I swung by his parents' place on the way home from our honeymoon and she volunteered to critique our wedding.

The funny part was that we'd gotten along so well before I married Dick. But in time, her no-nonsense nature and my tender Welsh bones collided. And kept colliding.

I couldn't shine floors like she could; I let weeds grow along

15

the fence; we had too many cats; kids too close together; and alas, I'd married her only child. Somehow, I could never see past the blunt words to appreciate her tender heart, and so I personalized all her comments, denied and buried my hurt and emotionally distanced myself from her for thirty years.

Every so often, I'd ask the Lord to mend the relationship. I'd mentally hoist the white flag and wave the olive branch her way—all overtures that, from my perspective, were flatly ignored. I compared myself to a swimmer diving into icy water and repeatedly crawling toward shore, near death with hypothermia. Even Dick couldn't grasp my struggles, and his best efforts at consolation, "Ah, that's just Mom," never satisfied my expectation nor salved the open wound.

Finally, I decided I'd used up my "risk quota." My relationship with Nana stalemated at politeness, formality, even comfort from time to time, but never openness.

Just before this last trip to see Nana, the old wound surfaced again as unresolved things do. I inadvertently spilled my need for help with a relationship during prayer-request time at a women's Bible study. "I feel like I've turned myself inside out to extend forgiveness to someone, but there's still a hook in me. I cannot get free of it," I told them.

The leader patiently drew me out. "Can you tell us how you felt when this person first hurt you?"

The accumulated "stuff" in my gunnysack of hurts emptied out in front of caring, supportive, confidential women. Then came the surgeon's probe: "Carol, do you suppose you became defensive when you felt attacked?"

"Defensive? Of course." Without thinking, I spoke the self-incriminating words: "But I was right."

The diagnosis continued. "By holding on to your rightness, you've blocked the forgiveness you want. Would you be willing to lay your rightness down?"

Would I? Jesus had patiently waited me out. I'd taken a

long ride—through Frustration Corner, past Hurting Junction, to the end of the line at Desperation City. I was ready for healing. More than ready. So was Jesus. Supernaturally, He exchanged my repentance for His peace. He could have dismantled the wall I'd erected between Nana and me with a celestial jackhammer, but instead He did it invisibly, quietly in my heart. But He did it. And I knew it.

Nana liked the rose I gave her when I returned from my walk: a deep scarlet-pink rose with a vibrant yellow center—and a fragrance to match. "Oh, for me? You shouldn't have done it, but you know, I haven't had flowers for years." She fussed with the baby's breath until she was satisfied and moved the bud vase from the desk to the kitchen table and back. Then she, who never initiated a hug and stiffened when others did, risked hugging me as Dick and I said our good-byes. Her parting words were, "Thanks again for the flowers."

Two weeks later, we made another trip across the mountains—a painful trip. After a massive heart attack, Nana had quietly exited this world and entered into her eternal rest. The florist quizzed me when I ordered flowers for the memorial service and a spray for the casket.

"Weren't you in here a couple of weeks ago? You were so eager to get just the right rose for your elderly mother-in-law. I remember thinking how lucky she was to get it while she was still alive. Sometimes little fusses crop up in families, and our pride gets in the way. If we wait too long, our loved ones can die not knowing we really care."

I nodded. "That can happen."

"But not your mother-in-law. That little lady knew you loved her."

"Yeah, she did," I said. She knew.

Loving an Old Friend

A local newspaper columnist recently described a beautiful reconciliation he and his wife had with an old friend.

His wife, Margaret, was ill with cancer, and together they agreed to pursue getting back with a dear old friend. The separation spanned fourteen years, and Margaret, tired of the hard feelings, wanted to see the friendship mended.

The wrench in their relationship hadn't come overnight. Margaret had literally grown up with her friend. Larry had met her in his early twenties, and for many years they both enjoyed a warm and deep friendship with her. A point came in their relationship, however, when things began to change. The old friend seemed to be headed in a different direction; communication became awkward and strained. Worse than that, they felt she was too bossy and judgmental about others. The differences finally became irresolvable, and the relationship ruptured. They could not continue to be together. Yet they'd been friends for a long time, and it hurt to be separated.

Larry described their disappointment: "Frankly, I was angry," he admitted. "My feelings simmered along, undealt with through the years, finally degenerating into bitterness. I felt like I'd been blatantly betrayed." Although time gradually eased the intensity of their feelings, they continued the estrangement.

Wrestling with cancer, however, raised all sorts of new issues—including the lengthy alienation from their friend. The time had come, they decided, to reach out to her in peace. Mutual friends brought them up to date on what she'd been doing over the past years. As they listened, Larry and Margaret found themselves not only curious, but also less critical and more understanding and compassionate about her human failings.

Finally, they decided to meet again. The surprise was that she extended herself to them immediately. They felt it when they walked in the door. She offered them forgiveness and love. She even gave them bread and wine, and they gratefully took it from her. A reconciliation had been effected and they were ecstatic to be back with their old friend, *the Church*.

The story reaches me. It stirs recollections of my own joys and frustrations over the years in relationship with the Church. Do you have similar memories? Those times growing up when you heard your first stories about Jesus from the lips of a dedicated Sunday school teacher. When you sat in rows and learned Bible verses and stood to sing, "Jesus Loves Me." Maybe the Lord's presence first became real to you through the Word preached by a faithful pastor. Or perhaps the example of an unpretentious saint, weeding the church flowerbeds imprinted the image of a servant's heart indelibly on your own.

The Church was a place where we felt at home. Here we sensed the goodness of God, not only through the worship and teaching of the Scriptures, but also through the variety of God's people and their gifts as we rubbed shoulders with them Sunday after Sunday. As we laughed and cried with them.

Churches are filled with imperfect people, and that fact alone makes them sitting ducks for Satan's attacks. If they are making any impact for Christ and moving forward in the Gospel, they *will* have their ups and downs.

The apostle Paul knew these real-life struggles well and described them clearly in his letters to the early churches.

Things have not changed very much. We still have growing pains, personality conflicts, divisive issues, differences of opinions. Sometimes wrenching, splitting theological differences.

All of this can be terribly unsettling when we so count on the Church to be our refuge, our reliable spiritual home. How much we want to be comfortable! How much we expect. Perfection, at least. Excellent music, Spirit-led preaching, classes that stimulate our minds and stretch our faith, and people who accept and love us as we are. Certainly we need high expectations. We need a place to be fed and to grow spiritually, but we're naive if we expect "the perfect church"—one that will meet all our needs, all the time. That's the Lord's job!

That's why Larry and Margaret's story touched me. In the face of their own disillusionment, they became lonely, hungry and at the same time, sensitive to the struggles within the Church. They then dared to look inward at their own attitudes and judgments.

I can relate. Who hasn't experienced crushing disappointments from the Church or entertained unrealistic expectations for an institution comprised of human beings?

Resentment and bitterness in the long run are only copouts, fueled by Satan's applause. They have no place in our hearts if we love and honor Jesus who *"loved the church and gave himself up for her..., to present her to himself as a radiant church, without stain or wrinkle..., but holy and blameless"* (Ephesians 5:25-27).

God has chosen to work through His people, which includes local churches, to bless the whole world through their witness of His redeeming love. Criticism is the easy course— that and running away mad. But we have other options: to be the Lord's agents of reconciliation, to pray for our churches and our pastors, to be honest, open and forgiving, committed to strengthening our relationship with the Church.

The Church was there for Margaret when she died. The familiar words of promise and the hope of the resurrection were spoken once again. There, in the midst of other believers, Larry heard the words as comfort from the Lord and felt deep gratitude to his friend, the *Church*.

CHAPTER TWO

A
Touch
of
Love

We love because he first loved us.

1 John 4:19

Midnight Ice Cream

I was in bed, lights off, but not asleep. After all, what eight-year-old kid would miss an eaves-dropping opportunity like this? Six adults in one place. And all within the range of *my* ears.

Tonight would be rich pickings. Two aunts, two uncles, plus my grandparents were about to gather in the little dining room next to my bedroom. I knew they'd be eating strawberry ice cream, but for me, missing dessert paled at the prospect of "savoring" private adult conversation. From my bed, I'd be privy to my own choice tidbits—family secrets, jokes, neighborhood news—all the stuff adults lower their voices and raise their eyebrows over when kids are around.

I didn't know it then, but what I really wanted was to feel like I was a part of a family, not just a kid my grandparents took in.

"Carol asleep yet?" An uncle's bass voice boomed across the room. I heard him pull a couple chairs up to the table and answer his own question. "She's gotta be asleep. It's past ten-thirty."

"She won't stay asleep if you keep making so much noise," chided his wife.

I wiggled deeper into the heavy folds of my comforter and bit my lip to stifle my giggles. Fooling adults was too wonderful for words. I loved it.

"Coffee's ready. Come on in." Grandma's invitation

Carol Greenwood

brought the clan to the table. They came quickly. Good people, comfortable, decent and ordinary. They surrounded the ragged edges of my young life like secure, giant redwoods. They deflected the winds and rains of loneliness and rejection that often swirled about me after our little family broke apart and my brother and I came to live with our grandparents.

How I needed them.

My city uncle, a great fixer-upper, opened the conversation. "Back fence is sagging, Pop. Those cedar posts don't last forever. Set a date and I'll be out to dig new post holes."

Grandpa, a man of few words, cleared his throat with a familiar low gargling sound. A long silence followed. Finally he answered, "Yep."

C'mon, guys. Talk about something more exciting. But they didn't. Except for the clicks of their spoons against their ice cream dishes and the sounds of coffee cups being refilled, it was the same old stuff I'd heard before: gardening plans, plumbing problems, kids' report cards and cousins' babies.

Then the conversation changed.

An aunt posed a question for my grandma. "Mom, it's been so long since you've seen your sister in Arizona. Why don't you head south for a visit?" I waited for her answer, but all I heard was a long, deep sigh. No one spoke. In the ensuing silence I visualized Grandma nodding toward my bedroom door as if to say, " I can't leave because of ... ."

"But you shouldn't have to be stuck here just because of the kids," my aunt insisted. "We can figure something out." Everyone around the table tossed out ideas that might free Grandma to leave.

All I heard, however, was one word—*stuck*. A perfectly good word, an innocent, shorthand explanation of my grandma's role as a responsible caregiver. *Stuck.* A word never intended for an eight-year-old's ears shot out from the dining room like a poison arrow delivering one message to my fearful heart: *I'm not wanted here.*

My fragile little world took another hit.

And my imagination went wild. The windows of the sunporch bedroom turned cold and icy before my eyes. The vines that brushed across the glass panes became sinister monsters prowling in the night, seeking someone alone and vulnerable—me. My chest tightened and tears flooded my eyes as a large lump formed in my throat. I tuned out the rest of the conversation and lay perfectly still for a long time.

I wondered if the Jesus I'd learned about in Sunday school had forgotten me, a little girl whose grandparents were *stuck* with.

Then, someone tapped lightly on my door and pushed it gently open. It was Aunt Adele, standing in a stream of light that invaded the darkness of my room and cascaded across my bed. I blinked in disbelief. "Carol," she said, "I was sitting out there just missing you and hoping you might still be awake."

At that moment she looked more like an angel than my aunt. A big-bosomed, freckle-faced angel with fiery red hair, carrying a white dish with a silver spoon in it. She looked me straight in the eye and handed me the little dish.

"Midnight ice cream, Honey. For you." I hesitated. "Go ahead. It's okay to eat in bed." She handed me the dish, bent over and kissed my forehead. "I'm so glad you're here in our family." My heart stopped racing and the monsters at my windows disappeared. *Maybe I really am home—and wanted.*

Why would a little dish of ice cream at midnight make such a difference to an eight-year-old girl? Why would I remember the incident more than a half-century later? Why? Because unconditional love has that kind of power, God-given power to affirm, to change, to heal a frightened little girl's heart, to impart the Sunday school message at a deeper level: "Yes, Jesus loves you."

Love Letters

When my dad died a few years ago, he left me a few mementos: his pilot's compass, a college banner, assorted snapshots and his engineering slide rule. That was it in the way of a tangible inheritance. And that was okay. The absence of material gifts seemed to enhance the real treasure, the priceless and highly personal legacy—my memories of life with Dad.

No inherited souvenir could have been recycled, replayed or reworked more. I've savored every memory a thousand times in these intervening years, the good ones and the painful ones. In midlife, childhood memories satisfy that voracious drive to piece together the puzzle of who we are.

Like I said, the memories were enough. But then, out of the blue, in a ratty old suitcase, something else came from my dad's "stuff." Something gathered up from his desk and sent along when my stepmother sold their home. Letters. A bundle of them, yellowed and stuffed into envelopes with old-looking stamps. Every letter I'd ever written to him was there, from the time I was seven years old until his death.

I will never again minimize the value of writing a personal letter. Or receiving one.

I settled at the kitchen table to read my stack of letters. Dick was working late at his office. The house was quiet. My tea was hot. An ideal setting for some reflective reading. Alone and still, the perfect time to be mentally jarred back to the forties. I expected to capture a new perspective of what it was like to grow up during World War II. Reading over my old letters, I assumed, would be like taking a benign cruise down memory lane. I never expected more.

"Dear Far-away Daddy, ple-e-ease try to come up for my birthday." The opener of that first tablet-lined letter grabbed me by the heart. From there on, I was undone, shredded inside by the pathos of the lonely seven-year-old letter writer—the little girl who happened to be me. "You don't have to bring a present, but could you bring my books, my paper dolls and my teddy from our old house?"

Instant replay: My old toys leapt to life through those words. But the real gut wrencher was the closing line: "If you can't bring the stuff, ple-e-ease come anyway."

After the first three letters, my eyes were too wet to read. I stood up for a breather. And to career around the room for a few minutes. I stepped on Felix, the cat, dumped my cold tea for a box of Kleenex and sat down for another "go" with the musty papers.

Nothing I've read recently has impacted me so strongly. Meager literary value, but priceless in helping the little girl inside come to terms with her childhood. Without these letters, I'd never have "seen" the path that led from "Dear Far-away Daddy..." to the high school version: "Dear Dad, I'm editor of the yearbook now. I can't imagine why they chose me. Desperate, I guess. It'd be neat if you could come up, but I suppose you're pretty busy."

Needless to say, this exposure brought a healing perspective for old wounds, deeper acceptance of parental failures, and, ultimately, authentic forgiveness. My dad, with all his struggles, saved a stack of his kid's letters. That, in itself, was a strong message, a love letter back to me.

In our busy society, not many people write personal letters—e-mails and faxes are lots faster. At a recent writers' conference, I challenged one group with the fact that not everyone will publish a novel, but we can all write letters. One woman later wrote me to say that her fourteen years as a legal secretary had taught her to prepare good business letters, but not to share herself. Now she was going to start writing personal letters.

Phone calls are so easy. We can instantly "reach out and touch someone" via the phone. I've thought lately, though, about the poverty of soul in a nation that someday might not have the enrichment of letters the caliber of those written by Robert E. Lee and Stonewall Jackson. These men chronicled their agony of leading soldiers in the bloody, divisive Civil War. They wrote of their devotion to God and to their families in long letters that continue to bring them and their time period to life.

I am glad the apostle Paul didn't have a telephone. I'm glad the believers in Corinth, in Colosse and throughout the Middle East could be buoyed by reading his vulnerable expressions of love, his challenges to stand firm in the faith and his admonitions to grow in grace. Where would the Christian Church be today without all his letters of encouragement and instruction?

I've saved few of the crafts our kids made. But, as far as I know, I've saved all their letters. One flittered out of an old book recently: "Mom, hang in there, baby. You're doing okay."

Letters. We need to write them, and we need to receive them. Not only because they record history and add depth and richness to our lives, but because we desperately need them as vehicles to share the love of our heavenly Father.

Letters. I'm so glad my dad saved mine. More than that, I'm glad my heavenly Dad wrote me first, passionately telling me from Genesis to Revelation that He knows me and He cares. I need letters like that—love letters.

Circles in the Sand

*W*hat I was hearing was no run-of-the-mill backyard squabble. The usually congenial and even-tempered neighbor kids—a sister-and-brother team—were engaged in full-scale verbal warfare in their corner sandbox.

From my weed-pulling vantage point across the street, I could hear and observe the whole scene.

"Stop it, Teddy. I want you out of here!" Five-year-old Laurie shrieked at her brother, Teddy, issuing an unequivocal directive: "You can't cross my line."

"Lemme in!" Teddy, three, was less sophisticated and his low voice more plaintive, but he was coming on strong in persistence. "I tell Mommy," he retaliated, at the same time slyly nudging one foot slowly across the Maginot Line drawn in the sand by Big Sister.

"I said, 'Out!' I don't want you here." Laurie's voice was louder and more emphatic. "Go play with your trucks somewhere else. You're too little, and you always wreck my stuff. I drew this circle to keep me in and you out."

You wouldn't call stocky little Teddy a pushover, but he was beginning to sound like someone who'd just been outflanked by age and cunning. "Me wants in, too," he yelled in desperation. In a last-ditch maneuver, he threw himself bodily across the sacred boundary line.

Teddy's action ended the cold war. Sparks ignited. Fists

flew. Legs kicked. Both kids screamed, "Mommy!" at peak decibel level. Fortunately for everyone, Mommy flew out of the house to quell the riot, close the sandbox for the afternoon and send her two tired warriors off for naps.

I went back to weeding, pausing long enough to notice that during my eavesdropping break I, too, had absentmindedly drawn in the dirt. In fact, I had etched a circle, one to keep the azaleas in and the Great Enemy crabgrass out. Though it was nothing more than a tidy botanical marking between the "good guys" and the "bad guys," I suddenly understood why Laurie had drawn her circle in the sand.

Drawing lines, it seems, is an easy way to distinguish the good from the bad, the desirable from the undesirable, the "in" group from the "out" group. On the surface, it seems like a convenient, natural technique to manage life and stay "in charge" in a world where it's a challenge to distinguish black, white and gray. Draw a line; erect a barrier; make a distinction. Get things settled into categories. Once a line is drawn, our fears can be shoved aside, and the sentinels "Safe" and "Secure" can guard our lives, allowing us the freedom to rest in confidence because we're comfortably on the inside.

Jesus confronted this when He dealt with the teachers of the Law and the Pharisees, the groups who persisted in using the Law to draw lines to prove who was "in" and who was "out."

Remember how they brought the woman caught in adultery to Him? They waited with bated breath to see whether He would circumvent the Law of Moses and ignore her transgression or whether He would find her guilty and encourage stoning.

As you recall, Jesus didn't immediately answer. Instead, He bent over and drew with His fingers on the ground. Could His doodling have been a circle? A circle would have perfectly illustrated what these Jewish leaders were trying to do—separate the sinner from the righteous ones by imposing the Law as their dividing line of judgment.

Jesus, however, wouldn't have it. Not then and not now. No law, not even the venerable Law of Moses, could be used to exclude someone from the Father's love and mercy. He silenced their self-righteous judging by challenging the sinless one in their midst to throw the first stone at the guilty woman. He refused to be hemmed in by tradition or the constraints of a written code. His Father's love was directed at freeing and restoring, not condemning. And this radical turnabout left them all speechless, unprepared for the triumph of mercy over judgment.

I've had to count myself in with Laurie and the Pharisees more often than I'd like to admit. Who knows how many times I've drawn lines or circles to protect myself or defend God's reputation? Yet at the time I never dreamed I was closing myself off from others or being self-righteous. I was simply acting out of "discernment" and "self-preservation." I quietly retreated, distancing myself and protecting my feelings.

However, I'm jolted awake from this pattern when I unexpectedly find myself in a situation where a circle has been drawn and, like Teddy, I am in the sandbox, on the outside looking in.

It hurts to be overlooked, excluded and judged. It hurts—a lot. And the only road out for us is the same road Jesus took and the one He continually urges us onto: the road that risks reaching back out in unconditional love. Next time someone draws a circle that shuts you out, take poet Markham's advice and draw a bigger circle.

> *He drew a circle that shut me out—*
> *Heretic, rebel, a thing to flout.*
> *But Love and I had the wit to win:*
> *We drew a circle that took him in!*
>
> From *Outwitted* by Edwin Markham

The Boys in the Locker Room

We did it on a dare. One afternoon after high school debate practice, three of us girls covered our heads with sweatshirts, removed our shoes and set a watch for the janitor. When the coast was clear, we darted into the most forbidden, off-limits place in our teenage world—the boys' locker room.

To our surprise, this masculine inner sanctum wasn't all that different from the girls' locker room. Perhaps the "fragrance" of sweaty tennis shoes hung heavier in the air and more dirty socks lay in the corners, but overall the two rooms were almost identical.

Talk about a letdown! We'd risked our necks to enter this bastion of high-school maledom, where no female dared tread, only to discover that the cement floor, metal lockers and square, frosted windows were just like ours across the hall.

Yet we knew that an unseen difference separated these two places. The boys' locker room wasn't only where boys suited up for games, but also, according to our older brothers, the place where boys talked about, bragged about, exalted or put down girls.

We decided that such chauvinism deserved retribution. We would sneak in, find the invisible macho mystique, grab it and run, striking a mortal blow to this male fortress. But the place wouldn't yield to our schemes. We found it to be a big nothing. Disappointed, we slinked away empty-handed.

Except for those years when the odor of our son Paul's

Carol Greenwood

tennis shoes escaped under his bedroom door, the memory of the boys' locker room had nearly faded. Until last week when my friend Janet rang me early in the morning.

"Carol," she blurted out, "the boys in the locker room are dead!"

"I didn't know they were sick," I quipped. Then, retracting my flippancy, I pursued. "Who's dead? What boys?"

"The boys in the locker room," she repeated. "Remember I told you how they'd plagued my marriage? Every time Fred and I argued about my wanting verbal affirmation or affectionate words, he'd dig his heels in, get tight-lipped and retreat into walled silence. When I pleaded to know why he refused to express his feelings, he always blamed the same culprits— the boys in the locker room."

I did remember. As a sensitive teenager, Fred reacted to the constant locker-room bragging. He was sickened by the tales of flattery and romantic words used to con girls into dates or press them for physical intimacy. He hated the unrestrained adolescent bravado—the raucous laughter, innuendos and dares. He vowed *he*'d never manipulate girls with words. No way was *he* going to tell a girl she was pretty or that *he* liked her just to get a kiss. Not him. He refused to be a hypocrite. He'd play it straight with girls.

Unfortunately, Fred's decision didn't dismiss the locker-room boys from his life. His anger only sent them underground where, like ghosts, they haunted his marriage for twenty-five years. He loved his wife. He knew, at least in his head, she needed to hear loving words, but he wouldn't say them. Afraid to be vulnerable, he retreated into himself while his wife grew frustrated, angry and desperate.

Janet's story was familiar. I'd heard it all before: "same trees, different monkeys." I call it the common wail of many women: unexpressive, silent husbands and emotionally hurting wives.

However, Janet's voice breathed hope. I urged her on.

"Six months ago, I opened fire on God about my frustration with Fred. I dumped a lot of anger right out on the table where I was reading the Bible. I reminded Him about Paul's admonition for husbands to love their wives. I asked Him why I had to suffer because some boys in a locker room said dumb things about girls years ago."

"And did you get an answer?" I asked.

"Well, yes. When I stopped yelling, my eyes fell on Jesus' words in Matthew 22: *'Love the Lord your God with all your heart and with all your soul and with all your mind…. Love your neighbor as yourself'* (verses 37-39). Familiar words, but this time they nailed me. They collided with my will and exposed my heart.

"All along I'd blamed Fred for being unexpressive, but now I saw another side. I saw idolatry—mine! Instead of depending on the Lord to fulfill my need to feel secure and significant, I'd groveled at the altar of affirmation, demanding that Fred meet *all* my emotional needs. I'd made him God, and he was only human. No wonder he resisted."

And the boys in the locker room? Janet stopped fighting them. And stopped blaming Fred for failing her. She was too busy setting her heart on God's love and loving her husband with new openness and acceptance. And the miracle—what the Lord knew all along—was that His unconditional, limitless love would turn her demanding spirit inside out and satisfy her deepest longings.

Satisfy and overflow. The morning Janet phoned me, Fred had taken her by the shoulders, looked her straight in the eye and said, "Honey, this is long overdue. I love you with all my heart."

At that moment the ghosts from the locker room keeled over. Dead. Slain by a Father whose love always conquers.

Coming Down the Mountain

*P*eter said to Jesus, 'Lord, it is good for us to be here. If you wish, I will put up three shelters—one for you, one for Moses and one for Elijah'" (Matthew 17:4).

Peter, James and John were on the mountain with Jesus. To be alone with their beloved Master was a rare privilege, indeed, but they experienced even more—the miraculous visual revelation of Jesus as the Son of God. No wonder Peter reacted as he did!

Who of us could fault him for suggesting that they remain in this heavenly atmosphere? Along with the others, he had had an encounter with the living God as he witnessed the transfiguration of Jesus right before his eyes. How could these disciples ever again contemplate the daily routine or the stresses of life "down the mountain"? How could they again be satisfied with walking the dusty roads of Israel, dealing with the everyday needs of sick and burdened people?

They had heard God speak—audibly. That's enough to make anyone fall facedown in the dirt. And that's what they did. Awestruck and terrified, the three disciples were laid low by the voice of Intimidating Love, Father God Himself affirming His Son.

I love this story. A mountaintop spectacular wedded to the mundane. First Jesus is glorified, and then He reaches out to touch the quaking men with two terse directions: "Get up" and "Don't be afraid." Not bad for men who would have to head down the mountain, who could not camp in the rarefied spiritual atmosphere.

A descent down the mountain was inevitable. Life on Earth was never designed to be lived out on a mountain peak. Jesus Himself led the way down, knowing full well, we believe, that mountaintop experiences do not comprise the totality of discipleship. There was still the ongoing commitment, the everyday gutsy choosing, the walking out of their real-life allegiance to Jesus' lordship. For the disciples, this meant that they had no sooner come down from the heights than they were immediately involved with Jesus in the deliverance of a young boy.

Whether it's the first century or the twenty-first century, commitment must follow a mountaintop experience for the revelation of God to have its full life-changing impact. From the Mount of Transfiguration to the Rocky Mountains, the principle is still true.

I wasn't on the Mount of Transfiguration, but I have been high in the Rocky Mountains where I was treated to a descent that underscored commitment in a beautiful way.

Three of us were wending our way down from the eight-thousand-foot level of the YMCA camp in Estes Park, Colorado, returning to Denver after a marvelous weekend retreat. Great joy permeated the meetings. In the grandeur of that idyllic setting, God had met His people in a stirring way. Worship was rich in spirit and song. It was tempting to stay put, to linger on the mountaintop with friends who were also basking in the spiritually rejuvenating atmosphere. But eventually we had to head down.

To make "reentry" easier and to savor the good time a little longer, we stopped at a quaint log cabin restaurant, the Fawn Brook Inn, where we could talk further about the weekend and enjoy a cup of tea and some Austrian pastry.

Our conversation would have continued nonstop if it hadn't been for the commotion at the next table.

"Don't miss this," our waitress urged. We all turned, eyes and ears taking in the scene at the adjoining table where a foursome, a younger couple and their elderly parents, were seated.

In a stage whisper, the waitress gave us a running commentary.

"This couple has been coming here every year since their marriage to celebrate their wedding anniversary. This is their fiftieth anniversary, and their daughter and son-in-law are hosting the party."

A florist's bouquet and a simple white wedding cake decorated the table. The scene spoke of commitment in a way no sermon could have captured it. The wife of fifty years continually flashed an endearing smile to her beloved husband throughout the meal, occasionally reaching out to pat his hand. He, meanwhile, sat silently in his wheelchair, staring blankly into space, while saliva droplets trickled down his trembling chin.

According to the waitress, a disabling stroke severely handicapped the husband five years ago. "I wish you could have seen him before," she said. "He was one handsome man. They were a gorgeous pair."

But the tragedy of ill health was not the focus of this day's celebration. There was reminiscing over times past, joyful laughter about the stunts of the children growing up, and gratitude expressed for the help given by the women of their parish in their recent need. This was no "pity party." It was a true celebration of love and faithfulness.

Commitment! Fifty years ago a marriage covenant was established, a promise of love for better or worse, richer or poorer, in sickness and in health. Surely, this couple had had mountaintop experiences during their fifty years together, but underneath it all some significant choices had committed them to each other for a lifetime. This lovely wife was living out her choice to honor this commitment, even in what must have been one of life's difficult valleys.

Joy—contagious joy—surrounded this little gathering. Most of the patrons in The Fawn Brook Inn that afternoon left with moist eyes. We did.

It's one thing to celebrate the mountaintops. It's another to come down and daily embrace the ongoing commitment of God's call. We saw both sides of His call that day—joy unspeakable on the mountaintop and loving commitment in the valley.

Like the disciples, we needed that full picture.

Being Somebody

We've never regretted living across the street from an elementary school. Oh, sure, from time to time there have been a few incidents—like a baseball or two zinging through the upstairs bedroom window or tulips trampled to death when the fifth-grade "scientists" retrieved their rocket project from our backyard. But over the years, the benefits have far outweighed any negatives.

Not only did our four children have a glorious kite-flying, ball-tossing, safe field to play on, but we were also treated to the laughter and squeals of hundreds of other kids doing what kids do best—playing.

Pretending, inventing, racing, singing, yelling—their noise rarely bothered us. Rather, it warmed our hearts. I've overheard tender and expressive apologies at the end of a soccer game. I've witnessed kids cheer on their disabled classmates at special field events. I've seen teachers hug kids who always struck out in baseball. I've also heard heart-wrenching, plaintive cries. Like the one I heard from towheaded Edgar.

The news hit the neighborhood three months earlier—Edgar's dad announced he was moving out, and in with another woman. Edgar and his mom left their old neighborhood and moved to a small apartment. From my vantage point as a "sidewalk superintendent" overlooking the school playfield, I saw Edgar's behavior change almost overnight.

His wonderful white-mopped head had always singled him out on the playfield. Now it wasn't his hair that caught

Carol Greenwood

my attention; it was his new solitary stance. He walked everywhere alone. Kids no longer hung on him, begging him to play. Coming and going to school and at recess, Edgar, the once-smiling, vivacious third-grader, was now always by himself.

This went on for weeks, until one day I heard him emit a blood-curdling screech. I was at my mailbox by the corner of the playfield when his voice pierced the air. I whirled around and saw Edgar locked in his teacher's massive arms, shaking with body-wrenching sobs. Somehow, in the safety of Mr. Matson's embrace, the floodgates finally burst. Head pressed against his teacher's jacket, he let out a piteous cry: "But I just wanna be somebody."

It made sense to me. Edgar felt like a nobody. In the last few weeks, one happy eight-year-old had plummeted to a new low. I'd observed the onset and his aggressively irritating behavior that invited others to back off. His emotional isolation spawned a vicious circle of rejection, and the pain was nearly killing him.

I was glad Mr. Matson was telling him that he cared. But you know what I really wished? I wished Jesus would tell Edgar that in person. That He would stride across that field, grab that towheaded boy in His arms, look him in the eye, and in front of his classmates, say, "Edgar, My son, YOU are SOMEBODY."

While we might not have had the emotional rug pulled out from under us in quite the same way Edgar did, most of us relate to his heart's cry. We want to be SOMEBODY; we want to feel that somehow in this big planet, we count. We're not alone in this desire. The world is painfully full of people grappling with feelings of rejection and insignificance, searching for fulfillment to assuage their deep inner longings.

When we don't know "we're somebody," we're easily tempted, like some of our biblical ancestors, to cover our need for love by grasping for significance on our own terms.

Remember those Tower of Babel folks? They thought their

brick-and-tar edifice could lift them above the mundane plains of Babylonia. "We'll make a name for ourselves," they insisted. Little did they dream that Yahweh yearned to stamp His name across their hearts, blessing them and elevating them with true identity.

And Peter. How much he wanted to establish his reputation as Jesus' most loyal disciple. How much he wished his simple one-upmanship would earn him a special niche with the Master and secure his preeminence once and for all. Yet, at the sound of the crowing rooster, his strivings were exposed. God had the last word.

"Don't blow your trumpets when you give your offerings," Jesus told the Pharisees. Don't parade your pious prayers on the street corners," He insisted. He wanted to unveil their self-righteous striving, and teach them the truth that they, not their efforts, were of infinite value to the Father. He wanted a relationship with them.

"I want to be SOMEBODY." Edgar's poignant cry is all humanity's cry. How can we count? How can we find significance? What will fill the vacuum in our hearts? Ever since Adam and Eve, this desperate human search transcends all cultures and times. Without a relationship with God, it leads us to a dead end.

I've been in that place more than I care to admit. Stuck. Frustrated. Pained. Every time I've followed that old lie that I could earn my way to significance or find meaning and purpose outside God's love, I've crashed and I've crawled out broken and empty.

Yet, in God's economy, the pain becomes redemptive. Here Jesus rescues me with the truth: "Daughter, I don't love you because you're somebody; you're SOMEBODY because I love you."

And Edgar, I pray you too will someday know this truth.

Hound Dog Days in the Kingdom

I grew up on a farm with my grandpa's two black hound dogs. Nellie and Jerry were lean and lank and could track the scent of a wild animal for miles without resting—sometimes, hardly panting. Watching those two unstoppable creatures squeeze under the fallen trees and dive through blackberry bushes in their pursuit was, for my child's heart, an indelible lesson in tenacity and perseverance.

I'm feeling that same tenacity and perseverance nip at my heels lately. Only, this time it's the Hound of Heaven.[1] He's back at it, tracking down some "wild beasts" in my heart. He's cornering me, treeing me, loving me enough to get at my relationship with my mother.

Mother's eighty-five now, and in a retirement home nearby. I am her chauffeur, wardrobe mistress, check writer, social secretary and "hot line" phone answerer. She's losing her short-term memory. She tires quickly. Often now when we go out for afternoon tea and one of her favorite Danish sweets, her head drops down for a quickie nap. She awakes with a start, spilling her tea and saying in a voice the whole tea room can hear, "Oh, Honey, I hope I haven't embarrassed you."

"It's okay, Mother," I tell her. But she's hit the truth. For as long as I can remember, I was embarrassed about this little woman who was always different from the other mothers around. I remember how she'd pop in at school to visit, wear-

Carol Greenwood

ing a wild hat and waving through the window at me. When the other kids would snicker and say, "Who's that lady?" I'd just shrug my shoulders and say, "Beats me."

Emotionally fragile since a child, she played the piano and wrote poetry while the other mothers baked cookies and sewed play clothes for their kids. By the time I was four I was putting away groceries because she couldn't gather her things together in an orderly fashion. Early, on I became the mother.

She seemed to attract criticism like bees to honey—her mother, her college music professor and finally my concerned father joined the cacophony of negative voices that pointed out her faults and enumerated her shortcomings. Small wonder her marriage and her health broke.

Thank God the Hound of Heaven pursued her, that He was drawn to her in her need, not put off by it. Her faith and a loving church fellowship brought her a large measure of stability and healing through the fifty-some years she forged a living by herself.

And now that same Hound is after me. A nip here and there and long-held survival defenses are loosening up. Walls inside are crumbling. I have wanted that more than anything, and I know I need God's help.

The Hound came on Kingdom business on mother's birthday last July. I'd just packed the last box of sandwiches and cookies for the reception at the retirement home when husband Dick stopped me. "How long do you think this party will last?" A perfectly legitimate question, but it struck a raw nerve in me.

I snapped back, "Doesn't anyone care for this woman besides me?" Resentment writhed within me and my defenses flared in the awareness of my own lack of love. "I'm going out to the hot tub and I want to be left alone." Hardly the way I wanted to spend a Sunday morning—snarling at Dick.

Of course there were tears in the hot tub, a good twenty

minutes' worth. "God," I moaned. "I feel like I've been the mother forever. How much longer can I do this?" Patiently, the Hound of Heaven waited me out. Then He posed a question: "Remember how I've asked you to treat the poor?"

The poor? I remembered a sermon from a little Italian priest at a conference in Brighton, England, describing how Jesus always "shows up" when our hearts prompt us to give to someone who can never reciprocate.

"Your mother is 'one of the poor.' She can never give back what you missed as a child or what you want now. But when *you* give to her with My love, I can fill you."

Jesus had spoken clearly.

Instant tears welled up in my eyes. This sounded like the promise of a miracle: Love when I had none of my own. I took the promise.

I had the chance to use it in the next week. I'd phoned Mother from home and when she didn't answer, I drove to the retirement home. Anxious when she didn't come to the door, I finally used a master key and let myself in.

Mother stood stark naked in her bathroom, trying to wash her waist-length hair in the tiny sink, water all over the floor. When she saw me, she looked frightened. "Don't scold me," she pleaded. "I know I missed my hair appointment."

Before I could remind her that I'd promised to do her hair for her, the Hound's voice intervened. *She's one of the poor, Carol.* As quickly as they came, fear and impatience dropped off. "Of course I won't scold you, Mother. Get your robe on, dear. We'll do your hair in the kitchen sink."

I gowned her up, mopped up the floor and moved all the towels and shampoo to her little kitchen. I ran the water, adjusted the temperature, but it was when I put my hands on her head that something happened, something akin to the feeling Jesus must have had as He wrapped a towel around His waist and bent over to wash His disciples' feet. The Hound of

Heaven, this same foot-washing Jesus, brushed in close to me. Love came when I had none. Tears came, too. I sniffled as I massaged Mother's head.

"Got a cold, Honey?" Mother asked from under the torrent of water cascading over her head.

"No, dear. Just looking at your lovely hair." And without thinking, I added, "You are easy to love, Mother."

She pulled up from under the faucet, water dripping onto her shoulders, and looked at me quizzically. "Oh, do you *really* mean it?"

"Yes," I said.

She laughed. "Well, if anyone loves me, it must be a miracle."

All I could do was thank the Hound of Heaven.

Note: *As this revision of the book goes to press, Mother, now ninety-three, lives in a family-care facility close by. It's not easy to grow old, but she's doing it gracefully and is still being used by God to teach me to love. She's not always sure who I am, but she can remember poems, sonatas, scriptures and silly jokes. She brings me much joy. I told her again, just the other day, "Mother, you are a treasure and so easy to love." And it's true.*

1. From Gerard Manley Hopkins' classic poem about Jesus Christ, *The Hound of Heaven.*

CHAPTER THREE

A
Touch
of

Grace

*A bruised reed he will not break, and a
smoldering wick he will not snuff out.*

Isaiah 42:3

Sighting the Good Shepherd

She had a half-price coupon for a deli sandwich. I had a dollar and eighty-five cents. She had intended to hop out of the office for a quick solo lunch. I'd been stood up by a friend who'd forgotten our date. Recluse and orphan, we collided in the hall.

"How about a sandwich at 7-Eleven?"

"Why not. You wanna drive or walk?"

"I'll drive my van," she offered.

We were "on" for lunch. Hardly a formal invitation, but at that moment, for some reason, it sounded like high tea with the queen.

Yet 7-Eleven is hardly Buckingham Palace. It's more a hybrid of restaurant and store. Crammed with convenience foods, trinkets, magazines and videos, an intimate lunch is unlikely. No place to sit, no gourmet menus, just cases of steamy barbecued chicken and humongous deli sandwiches.

"I can't eat a whole one," she said.

"Neither can I. Let's split a turkey on whole wheat."

We plunked our money down on the counter, and while we waited for our change, in walked Jesus.

Now, hold on. We're not weirdos or even mystics. We didn't see Jesus—either in the flesh or in a vision. In fact, we weren't expecting Him, and as far as we knew, He was back

Carol Greenwood

in our Christian office, and we were out for lunch. However, when Love—unmistakable Love—appears, you recognize it. The Good Shepherd had arrived. Picture the scene:

An unkempt, burly young man strode in through the front door, brushed past us and planted himself in front of the counter. "Sylvia," he bellowed, "guess what?"

The girl behind the counter whirled around and eyeballed the guy. The next second, her hand flew out and grabbed his. "Hank, what's up?"

We froze midway in our exit toward the door.

And then, eyes wide open, smile bursting across his bewhiskered face, Hank breathlessly delivered: "Sylvia, I've been sober for three days." Like a preschooler giving his age, he held up three stubby, rough fingers and repeated: "Three days. Three whole days."

Sylvia didn't even blink. She beamed unconditional acceptance straight into Hank's eyes like a laser hitting its mark. One might have thought he'd just told her he'd won the Nobel Peace Prize or qualified for the Olympics. But she only spoke a couple of words: "Hank, that's great." Her gaze far exceeded mere congratulations. Silently, but emphatically, it said, "I see the real Hank, and I like him."

Despite the setting, we recognized it: The Good Shepherd was on the move, reaching out in love. And as if hit by lightning, we were struck down by the power of it.

I've thought often of Hank since then—knowing that, even more than sobriety, he needs a Savior, one with the *love* to accept him as he is and the *power* to liberate him from all his sinful prisons. And I sensed that the Savior, the Good Shepherd, Jesus Himself, was hot on his trail—even in 7-Eleven.

Jesus isn't picky when He wants to whet your appetite for His love. I've noticed His tracks in unexpected places—

56

the movies, for instance. Remember the award-winning film *Driving Miss Daisy*?

In the final scene, the faithful black driver, Hoke, comes to the nursing home to visit his former employer, the arrogant, wealthy southern white lady, Miss Daisy. She shuffles to the dining room on her walker, frail, stringy-haired, no longer encased in her cocoon of upper-class respectability, no longer sharp-tongued nor aloof. Old age has won the battle over her social pretenses, humbling her with loneliness and confusion. But on this day she is lucid—and open.

Hoke's eyes meet hers and fill with tears. He asks if he can feed her. She nods her assent. Then the chauffeur picks up a few morsels and gently puts them to Miss Daisy's lips. Grateful beyond words, she responds in her halting, raspy voice, "You are the only real friend I have."

Talk about whetting your appetite for Jesus' love! That scene wiped me out. And even more. It propelled me emotionally to another feeding place—the Communion table, where Jesus faithfully meets me as my one true Friend. Where He steps over my crummy pretenses, my self-appointed respectability and forgives it all, feeding me with His own blood-bought love.

There's something to be said for tracking Jesus' kind of love in unpredictable places. Especially if we let it smack our hearts and show us the caverns in our own souls. That God-shaped void that will not be satisfied with anything less than our knowing *"how wide and long and high and deep is the love of Christ, and to know this love that surpasses knowledge"* (Ephesians 3:18-19).

I relate to Hank in the 7-Eleven and to Miss Daisy in the movie. In those painful times when God exposes my neediness and strips away another layer of pride, it always feels like failure and death. In reality, however, it's the Good Shepherd "finding" me once again and rounding me up with His relentless love.

Indeed, it is the shepherd's willingness to go after the one that gives the ninety-nine their real security.

Kenneth E. Bailey
The Cross and the Prodigal

Playing to Win

*B*zzzzzz! The deafening buzzer drowned out all the other sounds in the high-school gym that Friday afternoon.

The place was packed, and the noise level reflected the enthusiastic full house. Sound reverberating through the gym was close to the ultimate one-hundred-thirty decibel level. But the commotion was understandable, for this was the freshmen girls' championship volleyball playoff, and the kids, along with their parents and friends, were fired up for the big event.

I sat on the visitors' bleachers, in direct line above my daughter's team and next to Betty, another team member's mom.

The referee blew the whistle, and the starter buzzer sounded. Our team, the Thunderbirds, and their opponents, the Chiefs, broke from their respective huddles where the coaches were dispensing last-minute strategies. With a rousing cheer, each team yelled, "Let's go!" and dashed to line up on opposite sides of the net.

The first game went fast. The Chiefs poured on the power in a series of direct serves and spiked the ball so hard that it was next to impossible to return. In no time at all, the Chiefs had nailed their first victory. Our "Birds" began to look a little droopy, knowing that they'd now have to take the next two games in a row to win the championship.

Both teams spent the first break huddled with their coaches. Betty and I saw our coach vigorously affirming her girls with encouraging pats on the shoulders. She must have sparked the hope that victory was still possible because they returned to the floor with renewed determination. Right off, their server fired six successive aces to the Chiefs' court with incredible speed and accuracy. For the first time, we moved ahead. And our team went on to win the second game.

The Thunderbirds were ecstatic, and so were their parents. But our comeback was short-lived. Only a few minutes into the deciding third game, the fire began to sputter. The Chiefs' first server earned them five quick points, and soon they were impossible to catch. Even when the Birds got the ball, they couldn't put it inside their opponents' court for a single point. The score was twelve to two. Our girls looked pretty grim.

Betty and I yelled our reassurance to them. "Come on, girls. You can do it." But realistically, we both thought the game was already decided. The whistle blew for time-out. The Birds scrambled into a huddle. We tried to eavesdrop on the coach's instructions. What could she possibly say at this point to turn the game around? But it was too noisy to hear much more than her urgent directive: "You will have to cover for her weakness."

We could hardly believe it: Our coach was putting in Karen, an excellent server, but a girl who'd been out for two weeks with shinsplints in her left leg. Shinsplints aren't dangerous, but anyone who's ever had them knows they're extremely painful when you run.

Karen limped onto the court. Standing tall at the serving

line, she winced for a moment, then slammed nine successive fireball serves to the opposite court. The Chiefs were powerless to return a single shot. Finally, after missing a serve, the team rotated and Karen had to assume the position right by the net. A vulnerable spot for someone with an injured leg.

We cringed as the next ball smashed right toward Karen. Before she could reach for it, however, three teammates were alongside her, tipping the ball back over the net. It happened again and again. Karen never had to move her painful leg. All she had to do was allow another girl to cover for her and hit the ball over the net. The Birds had come to life. And more. They had become a team, helping each other with every play.

Our girls lost the game by one point that day, but everyone, including the other team, knew they had won a real victory.

Had Saint Paul been in that gym with us, I believe he would have leaped up from the bleachers and cheered for the Birds. Think about it: He wanted nothing more than to see those first-century Christians working as a team. His words to them emphasized teamwork—God's design for the interdependence of all believers: the working together, the honoring of one another, the valuing of each other's gifts.

Those parts of the body that seem to be weaker are indispensable ... . But God has combined the members of the body and has given greater honor to the parts that lacked it, so that there should be no division in the body, but that its parts should have equal concern for each other. If one part suffers, every part suffers with it; if one part is honored, every part rejoices with it (1 Corinthians 12:22 and 24-26).

Just as the Thunderbirds discovered in their glorious moment, that teamwork gets results, so we too, desperately need to rediscover that teamwork in the Church gets results. There are no superstars or benchwarmers in the Body of Christ. We must all share our strengths and cover for each others' weaknesses. What is more, God *needs* us to be one just as Jesus prayed we'd be. Paul's words are more than a suggestion for simple cooperation among divergent people. They are a mandate for the release of God's power and the display of His love in our world. Unity is His only game plan!

Traveling Light

*L*ord, *I want to learn to travel light.* It was a per-fectly natural request after reading Eugene Peterson's *Traveling Light,* a challenging book on the freedom available in God's grace. Little did I dream that a firsthand opportunity was just around the corner.

The experience began when I set out for a women's retreat in Warwick, New York. My suitcase was filled with clothes for two climates—chilly New York and sunny Bermuda where I would go on to visit relatives. I arrived at JFK Airport on time, but my suitcase failed to show.

"No problem," the airline official assured me. "We'll deliver your suitcase to the retreat center later tonight when the next flight comes in from Seattle."

I wasn't anxious. Between the efficiency of today's computers to trace missing bags and the determination of the airline to serve its customers, I was certain my belongings would soon be on the doorstep of the conference center.

Joan, who met my plane, was reassuring. She was also confident my belongings would arrive within the next few hours. We headed out through New York City's Friday-night-rush-hour traffic, minus my luggage, but lighthearted and eager for the weekend retreat.

The next morning, however, my suitcase hadn't arrived.

Carol Greenwood

Noon came, and still no suitcase. I double-checked with the airline. The luggage hadn't been located yet, but the airline personnel assured me it would arrive by suppertime.

Meanwhile, the retreat was in full swing: introductions, icebreakers and joyful singing. It was an inviting prelude for sharing on the grace of God, the theme of the retreat. Feeling very well-traveled and looking wrinkled, I stood to speak.

By the second session we were focusing on the character of God, a Father who deals with us on the basis of His love and ultimate purpose rather than on our performance or what we may or may not deserve. It led into the basic message of grace—the touchstone of the Protestant Reformation.

Jesus' death and resurrection accomplished what the law and our own efforts failed to do: render us righteous before God. Still we, like the "foolish Galatians," are tempted to add something of our own to God's free gift. What a propensity we have for weighing ourselves down with excess baggage and bypassing grace! For holding on with a white-knuckled grip to our pride, our self-sufficiency or our rightness. We could all relate to that struggle.

Closing on that note, I phoned the airport again to check on the progress of locating my luggage.

Puzzled and apologetic, the airline agent admitted that the bag had not yet surfaced. Undaunted, I was still convinced it would be right along.

By morning I felt differently. This time when I phoned, the agent sounded pessimistic. "Frankly, ma'am, it looks like your bag could have been stolen. We've checked as far as Hong Kong, and we simply haven't been able to locate it."

Walking back to my room, I felt the impact of losing my belongings. I'd been in the same clothes now for three days, and on top of that, I was headed for balmy Bermuda wearing a wool skirt. Here I was a retreat speaker sharing on God's grace and I was having some very ungracious feelings—self-pity, discouragement, annoyance, helplessness. I couldn't do anything on my own to change the situation. Close to tears, I reached for my notes and Bible and began rereading Paul's words on grace. Flipping to Galatians, I spotted a penciled notation in the margin—"Receiving grace is 'traveling light.' "

I recalled Eugene Peterson's book and my desire to "travel light." *Well, Lord,* I thought, *this wasn't exactly what I had in mind.* It did, however, bring more perspective to my dilemma.

I don't believe the Lord deliberately imposes difficulties to make us miserable. We live in a world where airport conveyor belts malfunction and thieves steal others' property. We are not immune to the world's ills. Losing a suitcase is, after all, a minor annoyance in the scope of life's events. Millions around the world never even have the luxury of any change of clothes. Nevertheless, at that moment, I was bent out of shape over this and I needed God's grace. "God, help me," I stammered.

A tap on my door startled me. A young woman stood holding two lovely white blouses. "Would you like to borrow these for the rest of the retreat?"

"Would I?" God's grace was in the hands of one of His daughters. The blouses were even my size. I was humbled, grateful and delighted.

The suitcase never appeared. An inconvenience, yes, but it wasn't all bad.

Frankly, to bypass the crowded baggage claim areas on the rest of my trip was nothing short of relief. Without luggage, going through customs in Bermuda was a breeze. I enjoyed the ease of not having to lug a big suitcase in and out of cars and airports, or, strangely, not having to decide what to wear each day. Freedom took on new dimensions. Even joy.

When Jesus commissioned the seventy-two to go out two by two, He said, *"Do not take a purse or bag or sandals"*

(Luke10:4). The pagans, it seems, were easily recognizable for their "loaded-down" lifestyle. The hallmark of Jesus' followers was to be their simple, but absolute, trust in God's daily provision for them.

They would discover, as Eugene Peterson aptly notes: "Freedom comes from trusting, not from manipulating, from leaving matters to God rather than trying to be in control."

My experience of traveling light, I discovered, was like Peterson's: "It is persistently hard. Nor can I do it on my own. I need Christ and a community of faith."

"It is for freedom that Christ has set us free. Stand firm, then, and do not let yourselves be burdened again by a yoke of slavery" (Galatians 5:1).

The Trip to Thanksgiving

She wore her gray hair pulled back in a bun so tight that it puckered her scalp. Except for a white linen scarf encasing her long neck, she dressed in dark colors. Usually black or gray. Never pink or yellow or scarlet or any of the colors seven-year-old girls want their Sunday school teacher to wear.

Variety was not a high priority with Mrs. Peterson. Her dress and her routine never varied. Each Sunday she walked to the lectern, looked at her brood of second-grade girls, cleared her throat in a shrill, grating rasp and blew her nose into a purple handkerchief.

"Girls," she intoned, "we need to be thankful to the Lord. Let us begin with reciting Psalm 100." No surprise to us; we *always* began with Psalm 100. I did okay with the *"come before him with joyful songs"* part. I liked *"we are his people, the sheep of his pasture."* After all, I lived in farm country and I could relate to the value the Lord placed on little lambs. But *"enter his gates with thanksgiving and his courts with praise"* undid me.

For some unknown reason, when we hit that line in our unison ritual, Mrs. Peterson started pushing. Not physically, but mentally. We could feel the "shove" in her voice and demeanor, as if she signaled giant herding prods to drop from the ceiling and corral us like rebellious animals. Her forehead furrowed. Her eyes narrowed, blinking out invisible fences to hedge us in. I knew instinctively that Mrs. Peterson had again set out to make us thankful. I, for one, decided I would not enter any gates laden with her baggage.

Sunday after Sunday, she persisted. Sunday after Sunday, I resisted. Each time we hit that one line, I went on automatic pilot and bailed out emotionally, locked toe-to-toe in a defiant standoff. No one was going to make me be thankful. Especially not Mrs. Peterson. My stubborn will inflated my sense of power. I had triumphed over my teacher's strategy.

I can't be too hard on Mrs. Peterson. After all, her noble intentions deserve recognition, and for years I adopted her same goal with my children, trying every ploy I knew to produce grateful kids. First the obvious: "Honey, say 'thank you' for the cookie." As they grew older and their good behavior became even more crucial to my identity, I inflicted on them good-naturedly the old "gun-to-the-head" routine after birthdays and Christmases: "You *will* write that thank-you note to Auntie Sarah. Or else."

Their little notes may have impressed the relatives and even set a good precedent for the future, but as couriers of genuine gratitude, they probably missed the mark.

Things do change, however. Despite Mrs. Peterson, despite my own stubbornness, despite my misguided attempts to pound thankfulness into my kids, despite the evening news and scary headlines, somehow, amazingly, a gradual revolution in my perspective has occurred. I'd hope Mrs. Peterson would recognize it as the real item—thankfulness from the inside out.

My route to Thankfulness has been filled with more than its share of detours through Whiney Valley and Complaint City. Frequent breakdowns still occur on this highway and always will, yet Someone has been at work and my whole perspective is different. A difference worth shouting about.

A Rose for Nana

Subtle signs of gratitude show up everywhere. In big things and little things, without any organ prelude or theological prompting, I'm feeling just plain thankful. Sometimes I get blindsided when I least expect it.

I'm sure you relate. A sunset explodes across the western horizon after days of monsoon-style rainstorms, and the whole scene knocks your aesthetic socks off. "Father," you breathe, "You have outdone Yourself. What a Creator!" Overwhelming gratitude floods your heart.

Your granddaughter runs down the hall, open-armed and squealing, to you, her grammy. At that moment, the house could burn down and the garden sink into the earth. All you feel is inexpressible thankfulness for another generation of fresh, exuberant life personalized in your arms. "God, you're so good!" It could sound Pollyannaish, but it's real—this deep-seated gratitude coming from your heart via your toes.

A valued friend and mentor dies and in the midst of your grieving, you are touched with undeniable appreciation for the privilege of that relationship. The words come un-prompted: "Thanks for Alice, Lord."

You find your car keys, a shoelace, or telephone change at zero deadline. A couple in an underdeveloped country share their precious coffee and slices of fruit in their barren apart-ment. You cannot cheapen the moment with a casual thank-you. Instead, you let your tears and your silence speak for your heart. The list goes on.

I grew up in a tradition uncomfortable with "emotional outbursts," as we called them. A smile, a nod, a polite note were our tokens of thankfulness. I never dreamed I'd see the day when I'd say "Thank you, Jesus" spontaneously, whether in church at news of answered prayer or at the gas station when the attendant says, "One more mile and this tire would have blown." But that day has come.

So what brought about the transformation? The apostle Paul would say that "God has done what the law (or Mrs. Peterson) could not do." He pulled off an "inside job." His cross has exposed me—and continues to expose me—as an utter failure, yet accepted and loved by Him and empowered by His grace. The progressive penetration of that truth makes every day Thanksgiving.

"Thank you, Jesus."

CHAPTER FOUR

A Touch

of

Presence

*The Lord replied, "My Presence will go
with you, and I will give you rest."*

Exodus 33:14

Trauma in the Tube

We had only two days left to sightsee in London, and since no one wanted to talk about going home, we spent this particular morning eating in silence.

I reached for the last piece of toast from the silver toast rack, the inimitable trademark of a British breakfast. Without a word, husband Dick handed me the orange marmalade, sipped the last of his tea, folded his napkin and cleared his throat. Daughter Gail leaned forward in her chair, squinted her eyes and scrutinized her father.

"Well, this is a hunch," she ventured, "but my guess is Dad has something on his mind."

After so many years, I no longer had to guess. I looked at my patient husband who'd held up for three weeks as the lone male in our group—a wife, plus two daughters and a friend—and I knew: This man needed some space. The one who'd heaped luggage on carts in the train station, stood in line for play tickets, opened innumerable doors, waited outside shops and calculated our monetary snags now had our attention for his announcement. "Ladies," he said, "I will be spending the day browsing some old bookstores—by myself."

We cheered him on and added our own plans. The girls wanted another "go" at the British Museum, and I needed to pick up some gifts. An affable arrangement. We would spend a day apart and meet for dinner together. Only one minor concern: Could Mom handle the tube by herself?

A ridiculous question! I was adamant in my defense. "Look, with my carpooling record and my nose for finding missing homework under sofas, I'm not about to be outwitted by London's Underground. If two million Londoners can maneuver through the innards of this city on little trains, so can one American mom. Of course I can do it. Trust me!"

Ever the caretaker, Dick cautioned me. "But Honey, you really don't like navigating crowds, and you've been known to confuse right and left when following directions. Are you sure you'll be okay by yourself?"

"Family, enough. I'll do fine. I will be at the Russell Square Station at 5:30. And," I emphasized, "I may even be early."

And that was how we all left St. Margaret's Bed and Breakfast together, boarded the tube and "split" for the day.

Shops and department stores along Oxford Street were jammed with people—tourists like me and the usual London shopping crowds. Both intrigued and somewhat intimidated, I did my shopping nonetheless.

By 4:45 I had found Knightsbridge Tube Station. Packages in hand, I eased through the turnstile, confident of my homing-pigeon instinct. Just as I swung my head to locate the descending escalator, the onslaught struck. From the left, from the right, seemingly from the sky itself, the hordes poured in with their shopping bags, their briefcases, their umbrellas.

I was caught in the cross fire of the mass people-jam, bumped on the shoulder, elbowed in the back, knocked hard by a guitar case and shoved sideways by the bodies attempting to funnel down two narrow escalators. Somehow I got one foot on the moving stairs and hoisted the rest of me on, grateful for gravity and for a five-inch space to grip the handrail.

A Rose for Nana

I hung on for my life. This was no ordinary department-store-variety escalator. This steep two-story job was overloaded with skilled riders who aggressively pressed in, over and around. And then there was the noise. It was as if someone had captured all the sounds of London, amplified them and piped them into the tube station for the commute home.

Midway down I was jolted again from behind. I gripped my parcels more tightly to my chest. I felt myself getting dizzy and my precious glasses sliding down my nose. Like a tidal wave it hit me: Panic! *Can I make it through here? Will I get squeezed off, only to be crushed underfoot by the feet of hundreds of commuters? Am I supposed to take the Circle Line or the Piccadilly Line?* My head spun and my heart raced.

"Jesus!" How automatic, yet incongruous, to say His name aloud on the escalator. But in my panic I said it again, "Jesus! Help me, Jesus!"

Then, just before I reached the platform, I heard the unmistakable notes of a flute—beautiful, crystal-clear notes penetrating above all the turbulence. A busker, a London tube musician, was playing Bach's "Jesu, Joy of Man's Desiring," and his music filled that cavernous station. The sheer grandeur of that simple melody played in an "underground cathedral" swallowed up my fear. I lifted my head and rode triumphantly down to the platform.

Jesus was in the tube station! The same Jesus who calmed the terrified disciples on the Sea of Galilee was in the London Underground calming one American mom.

"Where can I go from your Spirit? Where can I flee from your presence? If I go up to the heavens, you are there; if I make my bed in the depths, you are there" (Psalm 139:7-8).

Where is the Lord we serve? Not far away, friends, not far at all.

Caught off Guard

I found a new green spiral notebook on the kitchen counter one day. I knew who'd left it there. After many years of living with a list keeper, chart maker, full-fledged notebook addict, I wasn't surprised at Dick's purchase. Besides, I'd just picked one up myself.

"Man, are you guys predictable," observed daughter Jane with a resigned headshake. "I think you'd have put the new year on hold if you hadn't gone out and bought your new notebooks."

She's right. Our record-keeping, list-making regime is too ingrained to scrap now. We're not going to miss a beat or be caught off guard by not getting our lives organized — at least on paper.

Notebooks came to our rescue a few years back. We literally woke up one day to the realization that we were slowly sinking in a bog of chaos. Between Dick's demanding job, the press of four kids' school and sports schedules, gardening and house projects and commitments to church and family, we were overprogrammed, underdisciplined and careening toward domestic gridlock.

One night Dick, who'd always kept lists on such things as the population trends of Afghanistan, the archeological digs in Jerusalem and the heroes of the Boer War, suggested we attack our problem with pencil and paper. We couldn't continue to let disorder rule our days. In the privacy of the den, we made our pact: We would not be victims. No more would life catch us off guard.

"We'll rise from this muddle and regain control," I declared, invigorated by our decision.

Then with a stealthy move, Dick bent over his briefcase and pulled out an object in a plain brown wrapper. "Open it," he said. *He's been reading too many spy novels*, I thought as I carefully unwrapped the package. It contained the first of many green spiral notebooks. From this beginning, nothing was off-limits for these little books. We listed everything that filled our lives—our schedules for the coming week, family concerns, plans and dreams for the future as well as long- and short-term goals, whether personal, spiritual or physical.

Those lists exposed us. They reached out and confronted us with our own admitted priorities. And more. On paper it soon became glaringly obvious that we needed God's help. Before we knew it, we were praying first and listing later.

Finally, a semblance of order emerged in our home. The extraordinary thing, however, was that while we finally seemed to be gaining a healthy measure of control over our lives, by the year's end, our notebooks told yet another story: Life was no longer catching us off guard, but the God of the universe was.

We had the proof in our notebooks. We'd documented His quiet forays into our lives every week, not really comprehending the full impact. We'd simply chronicled His steps as they brushed against our ordinary comings and goings. Hardly headline news or the stuff of miracles. Or so we thought at the time. Yet, at year's end when we read it straight through, the picture was mind-bogglingly clear: We have a God who comes close with His banquet of blessings.

A Rose for Nana

Take a look at a few entries from the year's list: the offer of a weekend on the Oregon coast in a beautiful beach house when Dick and I were both weary and needing time away; the joy of watching lingering summer sunsets with grandchildren snuggled in next to us. The list goes on: times of intimate sharing with family and friends; grace to confess hurt feelings and the subsequent joy of a restored relationship; the surgery nurse's reassuring words and her tight grip on my trembling hand; sermons that seemed to single me out with hope, conviction or words of affirmation.

I could go on. Someone else might call them serendipitous, but I can't. Somehow they bore the unmistakable stamp of our Father's heart for His kids. Blessings that were undeserved, unexpected and precision-timed. I have to believe the Lord was, as usual, on hand, surprising us with evidence of His caring love.

We may have tried to organize and control our lives, but we couldn't corral God! It is as if He majors in catching this world off guard. Also in giving His beloved children new eyes and new hearts to grasp the truth that He is *always* present. And that His Kingdom is always breaking through to our world.

He sent His Son to us via an unknown, uneducated teenage girl who gave birth in a dirty cave. Then He announced this great news to a group of motley shepherds, the society's lowest, most humble group. He used twelve ordinary men to be the first to pass on Jesus' teaching. And in a culture averse to women, and especially to prostitutes, He illustrated His most profound teaching on love and service in His encounters with them. He turned the tables on the religious elite, punching holes in their self-righteousness to give us a true picture of mercy. Even death could not silence His love.

Our little green notebooks have ushered in some healthy

order and control in our home. I heartily recommend them. But I look forward to another year when the Lord will continue to catch us off guard with His unpredictable, undeserved and unrelenting faithfulness.

God at the Supermarket

*D*oes your carpet need shampooing? Have you considered vinyl windows? How long since you've had your chimney cleaned? Thought about aluminum siding for your home?

Sound familiar? Probably does. If you own a telephone, you'll be solicited for charities and political causes as well as products and services. And, if your house is like our house is, more often than not, the calls hit at prime time—dinner hour. I average at least four or five such calls a week.

Typically, I'm stir-frying veggies or grating cheese for pizza when the phone rings. The interruptions, by now, have triggered a conditioned response. I wipe my hands across the sides of my apron, head for the phone and answer less than enthusiastically.

Undaunted by my lack of cordiality, the salesperson plunges ahead with the latest pitch: "This is our finest offer. Prices will never be this low again." On and on it goes.

Like a robot, I come in on cue for this routine, "I'm sorry. We're not interested. Thank you."

Back at the stove, I resume dinner preparations while speculating about my caller. *What's this person on the other end of the line really like? How does she cope with the continual rejection she gets?*

Carol Greenwood

One Tuesday at 6:15 p.m., I received three calls back-to-back. Carpet cleaning. Vinyl windows. Pest control. (I must admit that last one was tempting.) I'd barely returned to stir the simmering soup when the phone rang again. Wooden spoon in hand, I retraced my steps, grabbed the receiver and growled, "Hello."

"Carol, I hate to bother you at dinnertime, but I've gotta tell you what happened to me today. I'll only take a few minutes."

I recognized the voice of my friend Jackie. She sounded upbeat, almost joyful.

"Our soup can wait, Jackie. Tell me, what's up?"

"You may think this is far-out, but, believe me, it's true. Today while I was walking behind the university stadium on the path near the lake, so help me, Carol, God spoke to me."

What a change from hearing the pitch about clogged chimneys and aluminum siding that never needs paint! This was a call worth answering; it sounded like a breakthrough in Jackie's long stint of illness and depression. I encouraged her to go on. "What did God say?"

"Well, it wasn't an audible voice or anything dramatic. I was walking by where the ducks congregate at the edge of the lake. I wasn't praying or even thinking spiritual thoughts. Out of the blue, the quiet presence of the Lord surrounded me. My ears didn't hear it, but my heart was flooded with an indescribable wave of love accompanied by the simple message, 'Jackie, I love you.' Has this ever happened to you?"

I hesitated. More than once I'd been told how offensive Christians were with their insistence that God had just spoken to them. I know people, in fact, who are so turned off by the words "God told me" that they reject out-of-hand all the Holy Spirit's works in personally communicating the reality of Jesus' love.

The truth is we do have a God who longs to communicate with us, who works day and night getting His message out: He loves us! He is, in fact, relentless and stubborn in His persistence.

Jackie pressed me for an answer. I briefly told her of the afternoon in the supermarket several years ago when I sensed the Lord's breaking through a long spiritually dry and emotionally discouraging season to impress me with three little words: "I love you."

Like Jackie, I wasn't doing anything unusual, just standing in front of the canned fish debating whether to buy tuna or splurge on crab. Also like Jackie, I heard no audible voice, yet the inner impression was so strong I whirled around to see who had spoken. While I rarely mention it, I have never forgotten it. What is more, I believe the truth of it to this day— I "heard" the Lord.

Neither of these two incidents—Jackie's nor mine—should be used to suggest the norm for our believing God loves us. In fact, we'd best stand guard against the devastating practice of demanding an experience to justify our faith. We are only too well aware of our propensity for emotional ups and downs. Experience can be ambiguous, and we are called to be people of faith, believers of the Word.

However, there's another side to this coin. God's message is so much greater than the condemning ones we often give our own hearts. He is committed to override the fears, the lies and the unbelief that assail us. When He determines to speak to His people, He does it—through a burning bush, through His prophets, through His creation, through His Son, through Scripture and, yes, through a still small voice.

It's quite possible, I believe, in a world where impersonal dinnertime phone calls intrude into our homes and where we mentally replay old negative tapes about our self-worth, that the Lord of the universe commissions the Holy Spirit to give us His message—"I love you."

It can happen down by the lake or even in the aisle of the supermarket.

CHAPTER FIVE

A
Touch
of
Faith

Let us hold unswervingly to the hope we profess, for he who promised is faithful.

Hebrews 10:23

A Four-Legged Sermon

*I*f you're a dog lover, you'll bite on this one. One Sunday afternoon on our walk around Green Lake, husband Dick and I bumped into a most unforgettable dog.

We didn't actually collide with this creature. In fact, we weren't even formally introduced. It wasn't, "Carol and Dick, this is Fido; Fido, these are the Greenwoods." No words were exchanged, not even with the young man who gripped the leash of this canine wonder as he walked past us on the crowded blacktop trail.

This little creature was unlike any dog we'd ever seen. In fact, we turned and stared in disbelief as he disappeared around the bend behind us.

Strange is hardly an appropriate word for any of God's creatures, but this dog was definitely unusual. He was no recognizable breed, a canine brand X. Head, shoulders, torso and legs came out of some pit-bull gene pool. But not his tail. Long and rat-like, it swished back and forth like an overzealous windshield wiper. Add his extraordinary coloring to "the mix," and you can begin to understand why his image stuck in our minds.

He was white with at least ten dozen black spots sprinkled all over, looking like he had on a Dalmatian coat, seemingly pulled and stretched to fit his short, pudgy, non-Dalmatian body. Somehow he had slipped past quality control and emerged just plain goofy. Any dog lover who counted success as owning a fancy pedigreed animal would lose on this one. No dog-show blue ribbons in his future.

I woke up the next day still thinking about this crazy little dog, and I have thought of him off and on ever since. I've recalled the questions other walkers gasped: "Where'd he come from—another country?" "Is he a circus dog?" I had their same curiosity and no answers. All I can tell you is that from our ten-second passing, I ended up with a four-legged sermon, something theologians would say transpired in a *kairos* moment.

Permit me to share it with you.

When we first saw this creature trotting toward us, I was too dumbfounded to speak. After my initial shock, I felt like shouting back at him, "You look silly!" But I couldn't do it; I was hooked by his demeanor. Sure, he was weird looking, but in that brief passing there was something irresistibly winsome about this little dog.

It was the way he walked—confident, secure, poised, disciplined. For all our gasps, snickers and stares, he seemed to think he was an "okay" dog.

This picture dogged me (pardon the pun) for several days. Why did it fascinate me? Why didn't I simply forget the silly dog? Was I becoming like a "dog with a bone" over some meaningless incident? Not so, it turned out. Foolishness was at work confounding the wise in the upside-down world of God's Kingdom. The *kairos* moment unfolded, and I got a sermon.

Here was a reject, a deficient dog who chose to believe that if the guy on the end of the leash, the one who owned him, loved him, nothing else mattered. I don't know how he knew it, but he did. Probably the heavens did not open and he did not hear a voice saying, "This is my beloved dog, in whom I am well pleased." Still, love had transferred—from owner to dog and back to owner. And the miracle spread: Love spilled out to others.

The master's love covered all the dog's shortcomings. They weren't even part of the equation. This little mutt must have received so much love that chasing cats up trees and digging for bones in flowerbeds paled in comparison with walking with his master.

What the world would scorn as a waste-of-space dog emerged as a testimony to a master's transforming love. Love was the fuel that pumped his doggie heart and energized him from within. Someone really loved him and he knew it. And what is more, it pointed me to the covenant-making, covenant-keeping God whose love continues to transform me.

Jesus loves you, Carol. After all these years, haven't you gotten it yet?

Did I need one more sermon on the basics? Well, yes…and no…and yes again! I believe it's part of that fresh wind that's blowing across the Body of Christ—and across the world. *God is renewing His people in love.* According to one well-known TV journalist I heard, "We are in the midst of an unprecedented worldwide spiritual awakening. And everyone is talking about it."

These are not dog days in the Kingdom of God. The Holy Spirit is reiterating, underscoring, announcing quietly and not so quietly, in ordinary and extraordinary ways and places that Jesus is who He says He is, and that we are His beloved. Faith is being stirred, deepened and ignited in us to enable us to live out the truth of who we are.

[We] are a chosen people, a royal priesthood, a holy nation, a people belonging to God, that [we] may declare the praises of him

who called [us] out of darkness into his wonderful light. Once [we] were not a people, but now [we] are the people of God; once [we] had not received mercy, but now [we] have received mercy (1 Peter 2:9-10).

I don't know about you, but I'll take every sermon I can get that showcases God's extravagant love. Even if it walks by me on four legs!

Coming Up Roses

everal years ago I promised myself a little rose garden in the backyard. Not that we were bereft of flowers or shrubs—we had plenty. But like most families with kids, we'd landscaped our backyard with the usual Northwest fare—rhododendrons, junipers, barberry—hardy bushes to withstand the onslaught of stray soccer balls, the crunch of badminton players' feet or the assault of a ball-chasing dog. Now, in our empty-nest era, I could plant something more fragile, something with color and fragrance—something like roses.

At first, I wanted just a couple of bushes. However, each June when roses filled Seattle gardens and flower markets, my little dream grew bigger. In fact, even in the dead of winter when no one mentioned gardening or planting, my dream refused to hibernate.

Instead, it quietly blossomed inside me, propelling me to such covert activities as ripping out pictures of rose beds from garden magazines and fantasizing about hybrid tea roses.

Once I thought I could almost smell them when I looked out our sliding glass door across to the weed-infested, frozen spot where I knew destiny and my dream would one day intersect to produce a botanical wonder-world, alias my rose garden.

Red roses, yellow roses, prize-winning pink roses—the promise to myself escalated. The more I thought about roses, the more I wanted. The idea of an occasional fresh rose in my kitchen window no longer satisfied me. I now wanted roses to fill our garden space to capacity, and roses to fill not only our vases but our friends' and neighbors' as well.

I hinted to my family. "If you're running short on gift ideas, why not spring for a rosebush this year?" And, bless 'em, they did. Roses rolled in—three from our kids on our wedding anniversary, two for my birthday, an extraordinary red one from husband Dick on Mother's Day. The word was out: I was to become a bona fide, card-carrying rose grower.

One by one I hauled the burlap-wrapped bundles across the deck, shoveled deep holes for them, centered them gingerly, fertilized them thoroughly, saturated them with water and stomped the loose soil around them. Full speed ahead—roses! They now had to grow if they were to outdistance my imagination.

I could hear the inevitable "oohs" and "aahs" that would surely greet my first harvest. I could see my sick friends' faces when I arrived at their bedsides, my arms overflowing with gorgeous, fragrant roses. They would, I was sure, lean weakly on their elbows and gasp, "These are from *your* garden?" and then they would lie down, smile and recover immediately.

But alas, dreams and reality have a way of colliding mid-air in the stratosphere of our expectations. I'd had a big, beautiful dream, but I'd failed to count the cost. I'd promised myself a rose garden, yet I hadn't reckoned with the possibility of any problems.

Like aphids, for instance. While we were on vacation, they came in hordes with their ravenous appetites. Unannounced and uninvited, they feasted voraciously on my fledgling rose bushes' leaves.

And dogs. Our own Wendy—the traitor—led the neighborhood canines in systematically digging for imaginary tennis balls planted in clusters under each rose. They exposed root systems, broke off tender branches and uprooted whole plants.

And mildew. And early frosts. And thorns that gashed my hands when I tried to prune without gloves.

To date, I've lost four roses, including "Sterling Silver," a special twenty-fifth-anniversary gift. Three others are limping along and will probably give us only a few buds this June. Bit by bit my dream has shattered, fallen limply to earth next to my pruning shears, my garden gloves and my dirty tennis shoes. Yet from the shambles of all my smashed hopes, I've learned something about rose gardens and promises and the power of the cross.

One morning as I stood wincing over the remnants of my pitiful little rose bushes, I remembered a song from the early seventies—"I Never Promised You a Rose Garden." I was reminded of Jesus' warning to His disciples before He sent them out: *"In this world you will have trouble"* (John 16:33). Yes, Jesus, who promises us abundant life, never says it will come trouble-free. He isn't out to discourage us, but neither is He after blind commitments that expect only blessings and are unprepared to put their full weight down on God's promises—and His grace—during the hard seasons.

I was getting a refresher course: Growing roses isn't a trouble-free project, and neither is following Jesus. We are naïve and foolish if we believe loving is easy, that trusting is simple, that forgiving those who've hurt us is a snap. No,

Carol Greenwood

the aphids, thorns and killing frosts of our little garden-worlds come in many forms—misunderstandings, hurts, rejections, ridicule.

Jesus, the Rose of Sharon, never promised us a rose garden. But He did say, *"Take heart! I have overcome the world"* (John 16:33). And on the strength of that promise, made in the shadow of the cross, we too can join the company of the overcomers, the folks who choose to follow hard after Jesus in every season.

Letting Go

I knew it was inevitable—if I were to keep my sanity. But I was the last to admit it: Wendy, our six-year-old springer spaniel, needed a new home.

It happened two years into our empty-nest era. Except for weekends and summer vacations, our kids hadn't been around to roughhouse with our dog. No lapping the schoolyard with her or placating her with nightly tennis-ball throws. Although Dick and I walked Wendy faithfully every night, it didn't satisfy our hyperactive "love sponge."

Wendy was lonesome. Hardly a reason to transfer a faithful family pet. Except., except lonesome degenerated into boredom, and boredom opened a canine Pandora's box of all manner of doggie misbehavior. This included tipping over neighbors' garbage cans, stealing lunches and baseball mitts from the schoolyard, taking naps in a neighbor's new car, incessant barking at the moon, scarfing down unattended pies or roasts and inhaling dill pickles and olives from the relish dish during holiday meals.

Impossible, you say? If you doubt me, ask my skeptical friend Diane who no longer scoffs. One night she popped into our kitchen just in time to see Wendy spring up on the kitchen counter, extract one chocolate chip cookie from the cookie jar and replace the lid. With Wendy, seeing was believing.

Amused? You're not alone. Our friends, *most* of our neighbors, the kids at school—everyone else thought Wendy was a one-of-a-kind, tree-climbing wonder dog. The funniest pooch they'd ever seen. Incredibly creative. And, of course, always lovable. I felt the same way. Except when I had to scour the neighborhood for her in the pouring rain. Except when I had to retrieve her from Duffy's Tavern where she entertained the customers by leaping for French fries. Except when I had to pry her loose from the junior high lunchroom on hamburger day, or identify her at the animal shelter forty miles away— on the snowiest day of the year.

Although I hated to acknowledge it, that twenty-four-hour-a-day dog was running in the fast lane and dragging me with her. Yet if anyone hinted that my life might be a lot easier without her, I either changed the subject or dismissed them as dog-haters. Privately, however, I sighed—deeply. After all, I'd grown up with dogs; they'd been my childhood confidantes. I wasn't about to let go of something that gave me so much satisfaction. I couldn't face the thought of living in a "dogless" house. So, for longer than I care to admit, I denied the problem.

Freckle-faced Wendy, however, never connected with denial. She was too busy living, being herself—one hundred percent. It would have taken a canine sleuth to track her down as she crisscrossed arterials, jumped over fences, even leaped through open windows.

But no doggie detective trailed her. Just me, one phone-weary dog owner, tired of hearing the same old request: "Lady, please come get your dog." The last angry call came at six in the morning. That was it. Enough.

I'd had it. The joy of looking into Wendy's big brown eyes for unconditional doggie love was not worth this kind of hassle.

Without a doubt, our city dog needed a country home. And I needed to let her go.

Does our God, Creator of the universe, have time to find new homes for dogs? I asked myself on the way to work. *Can He help one ambivalent dog owner part with her pet? Does He care?* I sniffled out my prayer request to some friends at work. Quiet, confident Laurie assured me: "God will find a good home for Wendy."

I could agree through my tears, but the pain began rolling in through my midsection. Letting go wouldn't be easy. After all I'd been through, I still couldn't imagine life without a dog.

But, wonder of wonders, my dairy-farm cousin wanted one. Somehow we connected. He needed a mature, kid-loving, non-cow-chasing dog. And Wendy needed what he had to offer—space, freedom and four kids.

I dreaded transfer day. We loaded Wendy into our station wagon and headed up the interstate in silence, she with her unsuspecting nose on my shoulder, and I trying to block out words like *meanie* and *traitor*.

Does our Creator God care about dogs and their owners? Ask me. I'm a believer. Wendy and the farm clicked. The kids took her to the county fair where she won a blue ribbon for "Best Family Pet." When I saw her swim in the pond and run across the fields with her ears flying in the wind, I saw beautiful freedom. "Go for it, Wendy," I shouted. And then we were both free.

When Jesus said, *"Enter through the narrow gate,"* (Matthew 7:13), He was describing the dimensions of our choices when we follow Him. If we opt for His love and His life, we'll get lots of practice letting go of those things that restrict our moving though the narrow gate into the spacious place on the other side. Into freedom.

And in His stubborn love, He'll keep moving Heaven and earth—and dogs if need be—to help us make those choices.

CHAPTER SIX

A
Touch
of
Truth

The truth will set you free.   John 8:32

To Tell the Truth

The whole room was mesmerized by the little woman in the blue silk dress. For forty minutes, Nien Cheng, with a quiet, commanding presence, told about her treatment at the hands of the Chinese communists during the Cultural Revolution of the 1960s.

I sat amazed looking over the crowd of four hundred people, mostly young career women. Fashionable, sophisticated, well-educated, most of these women, I was certain, frequently attended business seminars in plush hotel banquet rooms like this one. But tonight they seemed stripped of all their adult trappings. Like small children, they leaned forward in their chairs, eager to catch every word spoken by a diminutive seventy-four-year-old Chinese woman.

The irony was rich. The Joseph story all over again. From her cold, dreary cubicle in the Shanghai prison where she was interrogated and tortured for six and a half years because she unequivocally continued to speak the truth, Nien Cheng has been catapulted to an international platform where people now stand in line to hear her share her story. She has believed, spoken and lived truth. In that room, that evening, truth seemed to have a power and presence of its own.

"How could you keep your sanity?" "What kept you from just giving up?" "Why didn't you hate your captors?" The question-and-answer period was electric. The audience peppered her, determined to pinpoint the source of Nien Cheng's indomitable inner strength.

This wasn't a "Christian affair." Nien Cheng hadn't been asked to give a sermon. But truth, humbly and compassionately lived out, opens its own door for further exposure.

"I prayed. I repeated scripture I'd memorized. I was willing to die but determined to speak the truth." Her answers came quietly, matter-of-factly and seemed to fall on thirsty, incredulous hearts.

For two hours after her talk Nien Cheng autographed copies of her book, *Life and Death in Shanghai.* I overheard her hostess remind her it was late and that she didn't have to sign more than twenty minutes to make the crowd happy. Her reply was gracious but definite: "I will sign until the room is empty." The line was long, but people were patient, caught up in the evening's perspective of what qualified as time well spent.

The woman behind me struck up a conversation. "Can you imagine what would happen if we told the truth all the time? I can't get over how she did that—just kept refusing to confess to crimes she hadn't committed. I mean, really, it was great, but not too practical for the rest of us."

I sensed the wheels churning in her head. This whole truth business had hooked her. She wanted to believe it, yet her whole life experience told her it really wouldn't work. Not in the "real" world.

"You know what?" she volunteered. "I told a lie this morning when my neighbor wanted to borrow my iron and I didn't want to lend it to her. I told her it was broken. That's a lot easier than having your neighbor get mad at you. Wouldn't you have done the same?"

By now we'd inched up to within a couple of feet of the autograph table. Close enough for me to see the scars on Nien Cheng's wrists—deep, bracelet-like scars—reminders of the painful infections that erupted when her hands were manacled behind her back for days at a time.

I looked at the jagged scars and turned to the woman who'd asked me the question. The moment of truth had come. It was my turn to speak it—briefly, naturally, as much as this hungry heart could take. In this atmosphere, it was like pouring water on dry ground to say something as simple as, "I've done the same thing—squeezed truth, well, lied to free myself from someone's anger. But you know, Jesus says the opposite is true: 'Truth sets us free.' I believe He's talking about Himself as the Truth. He's the one who makes it possible—for Nien Cheng and for us."

"Really?" She was intrigued. "I wish we could talk longer."

I've thought often of this woman's question: "What would happen if we told the truth all the time?" In fact, I thought of it recently. I came close to lying when a friend wanted to circumvent the rules of our tennis club and use our membership for the summer—without paying the guest fee. I hated to disappoint her and her kids. They could have had three months of tennis playing. "Everyone's doing it, Carol. No big deal."

Everything in me wanted to capitulate to that eager, friendly voice. A voice that was soon joined by another, all-too-familiar one: *Carol, don't be a prude; it's only a small favor. You're not going to grow a Pinocchio nose overnight. The club doesn't have to know. You're not going to permanently scar your reputation.*

Scars? Scars? The enemy had overplayed his hand. I recalled Nien Cheng's scars, forged in the furnace of truth against lies. I remembered Jesus' scars. I remembered the price Truth paid. In the moment of my weakness, Truth came to my rescue. I opted for freedom.

"What would happen if we told the truth all the time?" That's a good question.

Breaking the Esperanto Syndrome

*I*f the word *Esperanto* doesn't ring a bell with you, don't feel bad. It is not a household term. Ludovic Zamenhof, a young Polish doctor, first came up with the concept of Esperanto, a universal auxiliary language using words common to chief European languages, in the 1880s. But any hopes that Esperanto might achieve a communication breakthrough across the world were dashed. Sadly, for the world and for Zamenhof, the idea never really caught on.

Now, more than a century later, Esperanto is little used and only vaguely remembered. True, a few books published in this language still exist, and several international conferences did use Esperanto as the official language. But the hoped-for, cross-cultural language revolution never materialized.

Zamenhof had high expectations. He believed one simple language could be the universal language, a vehicle through which people around the world could express themselves on equal footing. Speaking the same language would eliminate costly and aggravating misunderstandings and at the same time foster trust, mutual understanding and goodwill.

I haven't thought about Esperanto for years. Recently, however, my memory was jogged by a chance conversation I had on a flight en route to a weekend retreat. A businessman across the aisle volunteered he was heading east to address several seminar sessions of a prestigious group of business-people.

"And how about you?" he asked, observing the notes I had spread out on the lunch tray in front of me. "Are you going to a seminar, too?"

"Not exactly a seminar," I told him. "A Christian retreat—for women."

"Well, if it's a Christian retreat, for goodness' sake speak English," he said, with a trace of annoyance in his voice. "I can't understand the jargon and in-house terminology *you people* speak."

Obviously, a touchy subject. I sensed his adrenaline pumping as he vented.

He continued. "Pardon my forthrightness, but frankly, so many Christians speak an exclusive and rather archaic language. What on earth does it all mean? Your language is like a badge for the spiritually elite; no one else knows what you mean. You're speaking a kind of Christian Esperanto. Can't Christians break this syndrome?"

I couldn't just write off this young businessman's comments as defensiveness or an overreaction to some past negative experience, although both explanations were possible. The truth was, I'd been challenged to answer some hard questions.

How do we handle the Gospel, the best "Good News" in the world? The question occupied my thoughts during the rest of the flight. Then, as we prepared to land, my friend across the aisle leaned over.

"If I were you," he said, "I'd concentrate on telling your story like it is. Forget the gobbledy gook. Talk simply, naturally, clearly. Like your hero Jesus talked. No religious slogans, no cliches, no stilted Elizabethan English. And, wait, one more word of advice: Be kind."

A Rose for Nana

Talk like Jesus and be kind. I'd heard the heart of someone who'd felt left out of a "private club" because he was ignorant of the passwords and the inside spiritual terminology. Yet, at the same time, I sensed a fascination and even respect for the way Jesus communicated.

Look at Jesus closely. He preached and taught in the vernacular of the day, using illustrations and stories from everyday life. We have every reason to believe His conversations with friends were natural and appropriate—and, yes, fun! No ecclesiastical language, yet no compromising the truth. His words were (and are) loving and truthful at the same time. They penetrated hearts, challenged religious traditions and yet honored the heart of their intent and purpose. Not everyone received His message of the unconditional love of His Father, but not because it wasn't clear. Some of His hearers' hearts were closed and couldn't—or wouldn't—recognize love when they heard it.

The pagans in the New Testament projected themselves in loud and empty ways. Remember how Paul likened actions and words without love to *"noisy gongs and clanging cymbals"*? We twenty-first-century Christians may "sound" the same way when we slip into our exclusive "Christianese" and ignore the deep needs of those listening to us.

God's love is neither proud, rude nor self-seeking; it is kind. Spiritual jargon that fails to speak to others' needs also fails to communicate God's heart for them. Instead, it makes them feel like outsiders.

We can speak in the tongues of men and of angels, but unless God's love is burning in our own hearts and we are speaking simply, naturally, clearly, foregoing "special" terminology, there will be no real hearing for hungry hearts.

Carol Greenwood

What does it take to break the Esperanto syndrome? It takes a willingness to speak one language only: the language of love—simple, clear words from your heart.

Irresistible Forces and Immovable Objects

*S*tress—I'll never have to worry about that," I told my husband confidently several years back.

Never having had much more than a mild cold or light flu, I was unsympathetic toward "stressed-out" individuals and naïve about my own susceptibility. As far as I was concerned, I was not a candidate. Immune. Consequently, I was a little puzzled why so many people talked about their stress symptoms.

However, I now know something new. And, you guessed it: I learned it from firsthand experience.

To swallow my pride and "eat my words" was one thing, but to experience eight months of a painful muscle spasm in my back was another. Razor-sharp, unrelenting pain, the kind that eventually not only pierces your muscles, but attacks your thoughts and your energy. Life suddenly wasn't a lot of fun. And neither was I.

Others have experienced pain similar to or worse than mine. In fact, my personal adventure into "Stressville" wouldn't even merit retelling, except that the result was more than just the victory of a good recovery. It is the testimony of the Father's ongoing commitment to us, to expose our misbeliefs and to reaffirm the truth of His love, touching us at our everyday address, where we live.

The assault was gradual but progressive. An innocent twinge evolved into a sharp pain radiating across my right shoulder and into my chest. Innumerable doctor visits, medication, back massages, exercise, bed rest and much prayer didn't halt the persistent pain.

Finally, my sensitive, caring doctor, perceiving my discouragement, quietly engaged me in conversation. He began by giving me an example of an elementary law of physics.

"A heavy brick lying on the ground will resist budging under equally heavy pressure," he said. "But if the pressure continues long enough, the ground under the brick will begin to give way. Under continual pressure, force builds up and, whether a brick or a muscle, something's gotta give."

"It could be," he hypothesized, "that you're trying to move something immovable, or at the very least, highly resistant, and the something that's 'gotta give' is you."

"You mean like the old song we used to sing in the fifties?" I recalled the words: *When an irresistible force meets an immovable object, something's gotta give, something's gotta give.*

Healing truth at eye level where I could grasp it. A diagnosis in the guise of an old Johnny Mercer song ("Something's Gotta Give") spelled out the facts I needed to face. I was the force pushing against a couple of "immovable objects." Not only was I proving the physics law of force versus object, I was becoming mentally and emotionally drained as well. My doctor labeled it "stress."

What had started out as genuine concern for two difficult home situations had subtly escalated into a single-handed effort to remedy things completely beyond my control. My anxious striving and bottled-up feelings, according to my doctor, had put my body on "red alert," tensed and in a constant state of emergency.

The diagnosis, unfortunately, didn't eliminate all the pain overnight. Even healing truth carries a sharp sting. To face our own humanity, to be responsible for our own actions, isn't easy. It hurts to admit our propensity for controlling, our failure to trust God, our frustrations and our angry feelings.

For me, the stress attack was doubly painful. My back felt it, and my head told me, "You did this to yourself." The truth was that I apparently didn't believe God could handle those situations, so I'd taken up the cause myself. Anyone who's rubbed shoulders with a "Messiah complex" recognizes the signs. My own misbelief, prayerlessness and stuffed feelings had plowed fertile ground for a stress attack. And my back caught it.

While we may be shocked by our human failures and lack of faith, Jesus, the Irresistible Force, isn't. Instead, He is at home with our humanity, drawn to us in our need, loving us enough to expose our strategies and shatter our illusions that we can budge immovable objects.

His grace-filled prescription still administers hope and healing to people who know they need help, those who are weary and burdened. To them—and count me in—He says, *"Come to me, all you who are weary and burdened, and I will give you rest"* (Matthew 11:28). To me, that's an irresistible offer.

CHAPTER SEVEN

A
Touch
of
Openness

Nothing in all creation is hidden from God's sight.   Hebrews 4:13

The Bones in the Closet

Do you remember when spring cleaning was more than just a phrase? When overnight your home became the scene of domestic madness with Mom shifted into janitorial overdrive, scrubbing and mopping through the house chanting, "Clean, clean, clean"?

In my grandparents' house where I grew up, these house-cleaning campaigns happened every spring—and every fall. We belonged to that special "twice-a-year" fraternity. We were *real cleaners*—a definite step above the "once-a-year" people.

Daffodils signaled spring cleaning. And in the fall, the vine maples When the first yellow flower opened in the spring and the first leaf turned red in the fall, the "white tornado" struck our house again Walls, windows, closets, cupboards and floors quaked under the siege. Grandma scoured, sanitized, waxed and polished for two arduous weeks, using her special cleaning rags, cleansers and brushes, plus some elusive formula she called "elbow grease," which, I learned later, did not come from the local hardware store.

Boxes of stuff were carted off to the Salvation Army and the church mission barrel. Invariably, that great exodus always made me nervous. I'd go to bed and dream about gigantic conveyer belts hauling out the homey things I loved— favorite pillows, dolls, blankets. I worried whether my cat

Carol Greenwood

would survive the purge or if one of my special books would be snapped up and whisked away.

Our kids have no memories of twice-a-year cleaning campaigns, of beating carpets over clotheslines or washing every window in the house on the same day. They learned a whole new culture: countdown vacuuming before company arrives, emergency boxes for quick countertop cleaning, Saturday chores before allowances. They adapted comfortably to a "lived-in" look.

Besides not being world-class cleaners, we were, unfortunately, savers. People who hated to throw things away, people who reproduced more savers. So, when the last bird flew off to college, Dick and I faced the consequences of thirty years of saving. We moved into a major cleaning project, determined to be ruthless in disposing of our accumulated stuff. We made five trips to the dump, hired a man to haul away an old sofa the salvage people rejected and, whenever possible, stuffed our kids' remaining possessions in their cars when they came to visit.

Apparently the project hadn't been thorough enough, however. A friend dropped by who actually wanted something I was trying to give away. Eagerly, I took her up to daughter Anne's old room, flung open the closet door, then ducked as a large bag cascaded off the top shelf and crashed loudly at our feet.

"What's in the sack?" she asked. I understood her curiosity but was reluctant to explain.

"Oh, just some bones, that's all," I assured her and attempted to change the subject.

She wouldn't be put off. "What bones?"

I had no option but to explain that these bones came home from college, relics from Anne's anatomy class.

"You mean you're keeping *human bones* in your closet?" she pursued.

A Rose for Nana

That did it. The next day, I determined to get rid of them. A simple resolution but not so simple to carry out.

The garbage can seemed like the natural repository, and I had them almost stuffed in when Dick quizzed me. "Are you sure you want those bones found in *our* garbage? What if some dogs tip over the can before the truck comes?" He had a point.

I'd bury them in the backyard—the perfect solution. Or so I thought until I noticed Wendy, our digger dog, circling the area with an archeological project in mind. Then Dick raised another issue: Seattle's unresolved Green River serial murders, with victims' bones still being found in the city. Did we want to chance interrogation about human bones buried on our property?

The fireplace appeared to be my only answer. But as I bent over the grate, poised to burn the bones, I backed out. These were, after all, the remnants of a person, a real human being. A sense of dignity and reverence won out over expediency, and the bones eventually went on their way to a nearby college.

Old spiritual skeletons, it seems, are not easy to dismiss either. Shoved away out of sight, stuffed in our "keep-looking-good" closets, the bones of unforgiven sin, unresolved hurts or disappointments also have ways of popping out at inopportune moments, of falling out to call the shots in our thinking and responses, impairing our ability to love as Jesus did.

I'm tempted to shove stuff into my personal closet and call it anything but sin. Are you familiar with the pattern? You slam the door shut, nail it tight with some good Christian-sounding explanation and then before you know it you have ushered in a time of spiritual impotence and, if we're honest, hypocrisy.

Extraordinarily, Jesus holds us in His grip even in these times. He is persistent. He keeps knocking on our door again

117

and again, ready to haul the old dead bones out of the closet. He is eager to breathe new life into them as He did in Ezekiel's day, when God's people had lost all hope. He is just as eager to throw in a new heart and a new spirit to boot.

"I the LORD have spoken, and I will do it" (Ezekiel 36:36).

Jesus and the B & B

*L*ike so many turnarounds, this one wasn't dramatic. No screeching brakes. No skidmarks on the road. No harrowing U-turns. Just the handing over of two fresh brown eggs from one neighbor to another. A natural, ordinary event. So typical of the arenas God chooses when He wants to sideswipe our human frailties with His redemptive love.

As usual, He caught me off guard. I wasn't dressed for a profound spiritual experience. The radio wasn't playing Christian music. The scene was "early-breakfast—jeans-and-dirty-dishes." I'd just popped the last cereal bowl into the dishwasher when the doorbell rang.

Betty, my neighbor, stood at the front door with that "save-me-a-trip-to-the-store" look we both understood.

"No problem," I assured her. I knew how it felt to be in the middle of mixing a cake and discover you'd run out of eggs. "Stay right there, Betty, I'll bring you a couple from the fridge."

In a flash, I zipped down the front hall to the kitchen, grabbed two eggs and delivered them into her waiting hands.

"You couldn't get better service at Safeway," I quipped.

Then I closed the transaction (and the door) with the familiar supermarket seal: "Have a good day."

The ways of the Holy Spirit were new to me then, but my initiation began that morning in my kitchen.

Carol, why did you leave Betty standing in the front hall? Why didn't you invite her into the kitchen?

No audible voice, no spooky music, just a deep, clear inner knowing. Clear enough to prompt a response, at least in my thoughts.

Betty's a busy lady. She doesn't want to make small talk in my kitchen. She wants to get on with her baking.

Carol, what is the real reason you left her standing by the door?

This still-small-voice business, I was discovering, was not only personal, it was persistent.

Okay, Lord, I conceded. *I hear You. The truth is that Betty's a tidy Scandinavian housekeeper, and I didn't want her to see my cluttered kitchen counters this morning.*

Even as I expressed it, I shuddered at the sight of three encyclopedias pressing flowers, a stack of old magazines set aside to clip recipes from and a jar of peanut butter left out from making the kids' sandwiches.

Betty's counters were always *clear*—and waxed.

What are you afraid of? The questioning pressed on.

Enough, I thought. I quietly terminated the conversation. Not for long, however. I couldn't bear the silence of the kitchen and the unsatisfied feeling of stuffing an issue instead of resolving it. Besides, I was starting to feel something else—a pain in my midsection.

All right, I surrender, Lord. I'm afraid that if Betty sees my counter, she won't like me.

And so you defended yourself at the price of not receiving her. Self-protection isn't love, Carol.

Pow. I felt penetrating, pristine truth zing across my court, faster and more accurate than any tennis ball I'd ever encountered. I'd just been aced, but not by condemnation—by liberating love.

What does it mean to love people? To open ourselves and our homes to others? What's true hospitality? I've asked myself those questions often over the years since that egg exchange.

And slowly the picture is becoming clearer, especially after a recent trip Dick and I took through New England via all sorts of B & B's.

The hosts of bed-and-breakfast places uniformly amazed us. They literally "opened" themselves and their homes for our comfort and rest. One hostess in Boston had fresh flowers in our room, travel guides on our nightstand, hand lotion and extra shower caps in the bathroom, even a robe in case we'd forgotten ours. And like our hosts all along the way, she served us breakfast on "company" dishes—the family's china—and orange juice in their best crystal.

From Cape Cod to Maine, Dick and I couldn't get over the personalized care, how superior in thoughtfulness to most hotels. The lovely amenities, however, didn't ultimately captivate us. The people did—the openness of our hosts. They pulled up chairs in the dining room and joined us for coffee. They showed us pictures of their children or grandchildren, asked us about ours, let us see the kitchen and the rest of the house. In a word, they risked letting us "in."

Jesus must have sensed this atmosphere at Mary and Martha's place in Bethany. Apparently He felt comfortable there in spite of their imperfections. I wonder if Luke doesn't give us a clue when he writes: *"As Jesus and his disciples were on their way, he came to a village where a woman named Martha opened her home to him"* (Luke 10:38).

Openness. It is, I'm discovering, the key to true hospitality and real love. Sharing our homes and a couple of eggs is good, but if we withhold ourselves in the process, it isn't enough.

Jesus never kept people standing empty-handed in the front hall to protect His image as the Son of God. Instead, He emptied Himself of pride and aloofness and chose the role of a servant. He chose to be vulnerable, even to death. Real love, Jesus' kind of love, opens up. It lets people in.

Can we settle for anything less?

Out of Hiding

The September sunlight filtered through the trees on the Prinsengracht, a quiet street along the canal in Amsterdam, Netherlands. My husband and I stood on the street's edge with a group of other eager tourists, waiting to enter Number 263, the Anne Frank House.

Wedged tightly in a row typical of the older Amsterdam neighborhoods, this house stands out as a landmark, made world-famous through the writings of a thirteen-year-old girl. Millions have read Anne Frank's incredibly perceptive diary chronicling the twenty-five months in which the heroic Frank family and four other people hid here, in continual fear of being arrested and hauled off as part of Hitler's mass plan to exterminate the Jews.

For us waiting outside the house that September day, life was comfortable and pleasant under the warmth of the autumn sun. Jovial tourists struck up animated conversations, laughing and joking as they anticipated this stop.

From our place in line, Dick and I watched people leave the building. "Everyone looks pretty somber," he observed. I agreed. Their faces mirrored disbelief and horror. Then, we went in.

Immediately we were transported back to early 1942. That's when Mr. Frank started bringing in a few household effects, bit by bit, to the rooms above the warehouse, as he prepared to take his family into hiding. Shortly they—Mr. and Mrs. Frank and their daughters—moved in, joined later by the Van Daans and their son, Peter. The accommodations were primitive, and life restrictive. A heavy bookcase marked the entrance to the area. To even turn on the faucet or use the toilet before 5 p.m. when the employees of the office below left was dangerous. During daytime they drew the shades and walked on tiptoe across the rooms. A dark, silent existence for all of them.

The Franks and the Van Daans were bright, creative people, and Anne's diary records their valiant efforts to live normally in hiding. With ingenuity and determination to carry on, they played games, listened to music, talked together and celebrated holidays and birthdays.

As Dick and I walked from room to room, we saw their cramped, dark quarters and were sobered by the conditions in which they lived. Not only did they suffer daily deprivations, but overcrowding and bouts of intense fear as well. While this "home" was their only chance for survival, it was nevertheless a prison, and they were prisoners.

Neither Dick nor I could say a word as we left the tour. We walked away from the house speechless, gripped by the tragic reality that liberation had come too late for these people. Afterwards, our own freedom seemed loose and extravagant. Here we were, free to be gawky tourists and free to walk away.

Ever since we stepped out that door I've had a heightened appreciation for Jesus' ministry as liberator who calls us out of hiding.

Self-preservation is a powerful instinct in human beings. My first reaction when I'm threatened in any way is to hide. Like the Franks, I want a refuge. Most of us have never had to hide in the upstairs of an old warehouse or in mountain caves such as the Israelites did when the fierce Midianite army ravaged their homes and stole their cattle (Judges 6). Yet we can relate to other kinds of hiding—hiding our true feelings from each other, hiding our fears and weaknesses because we're afraid we'll be rejected if others really know us.

Living in a fallen world and inheriting a sinful nature has left us—all of us—vulnerable to hurt, disappointment and rejection. The fear of more trauma tempts us to run for cover. And, speaking for myself, that strategy always frustrates my true need—to be known and accepted just as I am—"warts and all."

Only when we encounter the extraordinary love of Jesus, the Great Liberator, do we dare to entertain the possibility of true freedom. What great joy to discover that the Gospel really is good news, that the Shepherd has been searching for us all along and that He came to earth on a mission to release us from our hidden prisons. Incredibly, this stubborn Shepherd can find us even in our hiding places!

But old patterns and habits are entrenched, and even after we know the Liberator we often fail to grasp the full dimensions of His freeing power. In our heads maybe, but not in our hearts. Our fears die slowly, and coming out of hiding, we discover, is risky business. I find it scary to rip off my mask and let you know who I really am. The greatest tragedy is that as a mask-wearer I cannot be an open channel of God's love to a hurting, desperate world. Moreover, I will not know true joy.

The world doesn't need any more phonies; it will continue to produce its own. What the world needs and what God wants are Christians who will come out of hiding, who will stand up and admit they're human, who will let go of pride, give up their self-righteousness, admit their needs and even risk giving up their fears of what others think—all in order to love. In short, God wants "real" people, ordinary sinners who've discovered the safest hiding place in the world is in the arms of the waiting Father.

Count me in with those folks.

CHAPTER EIGHT

A
Touch
of

"Fear not, for I have redeemed you; I have summoned you by name; you are mine."

Isaiah 43:1

The Intruder

August 12, 1991. The morning's reading came alive to me: *"He who dwells in the shelter of the Most High will rest in the shadow of the Almighty. ... 'He is my refuge and my fortress, my God, in whom I trust.' ... He will cover you with his feathers, and under his wings you will find refuge; his faithfulness will be your shield and rampart"* (Psalm 91:1-4).

Familiar words, certainly, but this particular morning they spoke with a fresh vigor of God's tenderness and protection. So much so that I copied—and underlined—them in my journal. When I got to verse 5, my pen and my heart both leaped: *"You will not fear the terror of night."*

That's it, God. These are words I need. They're designed for the heart of Chicken Little, the one who grew up scared of the dark and who, even now, elbows her husband at night to check on every little noise. I put down my journal and repeated the words aloud: *"You will not fear the terror of night." Dear God, get these words past my mountain of fear, past my analytical mind and into my heart.*

The psalmist's words got the litmus test for truth that very night—just after our neighbors went home from our backyard barbecue.

"News is on," Dick called from the family room. I put the last few dishes in the dishwasher and joined him on the sofa for the late TV news. Within minutes, a noise from the laundry room diverted our attention and we exchanged knowing looks: *our cats again, Felix and Ursula.* They often jumped off the dryer down to their food dishes. But, then our laundry room door creaked open. *They open doors like people, these crazy cats.* Or so I thought until I noticed Dick's out-of-the-ordinary quizzical look as he leaned forward toward the door. Our eyes met; we knew we'd heard a footstep. Someone was coming into our house!

Within seconds we saw him: a man wearing a nylon stocking stretched over his face, armed with a drawn pistol in one hand and brandishing a knife in the other. He moved through the laundry room doorway into the kitchen and literally leapt into the family room in front of us.

"Who are you?" Dick stood to his full six-foot four-inch stature and belted out his question. This was hardly the time for introductions or philosophical questions about identity, but Dick's query definitely broke the ice.

"Down on the floor. Both of you. I want money—now!" A string of loud profanity followed terse orders as he gestured toward the floor where he ordered us to lie facedown. Terrified, I dropped to the carpet, my chest tight and my heart racing. My throat went dry. *God, help us,* I gasped under my breath. *God, help us.* I braced myself against what I feared hearing next—a gunshot.

"I want money. All you've got. Get it now!" Like a volcano spewing out suffocating black smoke, the intruder blasted out another string of profanities, filling the room with an oppressive presence. He moved closer to Dick until the gun was only inches from my husband's forehead.

Then he spotted Dick's ring finger and the large diamond ring he'd inherited from his grandfather. "Give me that ring!" he demanded as he bent over my husband's prostrate body and snatched the ring.

My thoughts fell over themselves trying to sort out the reality of the present moment. *This is unreal; it can't be happening, not in our neighborhood.* But it was real, and the gunman underscored that fact when he yelled out his loud demand once more: "Get me some money now!"

"My wallet's in my trousers upstairs." Dick repeated himself at least four times before the intruder got the message.

"I'll go get it. I'll go upstairs," I offered, surprised that I could even utter a sound. But strangely, calmness seemed to be moving in on me in the midst of this terror.

"We'll all go upstairs," the gunman barked. "Come on, move!" We raced up the stairs two at a time. I led the way to our bedroom. Dick followed with the gun pressed into his back.

Dick found his wallet quickly. "Hand it to her," the man ordered, keeping Dick at bay in the closet once he'd handed me the wallet. I thrust it into the intruder's hands, and in seconds the yelling resumed: "There's only eight dollars here. You've got more money around here. Come on. Where is it?"

Dick and I exchanged helpless looks. "That's all the cash we have in the house," Dick said.

"You better come up with something more!" The man shouted and waved his gun wildly in circles toward us. My mind shifted to overdrive. *This guy's on drugs and needs a fix. He's desperate. What else have we got in the house?* My eyes scanned the bedroom and my search ended at Dick's dresser. *The gold coins in Dick's top drawer. I'd seen them yesterday when I put away his handkerchiefs.* The coins, worth about $700, were from his dad's collection. We'd planned to give them to our kids. "Wait a minute. We've got some gold coins in that drawer. You can have them." I pointed to the dresser near where Dick was being held hostage.

The man barked his orders to Dick: "Pull out the drawer." I grabbed the drawer from Dick and dumped its contents on the carpet. I glanced back at Dick, wondering if this might be the moment he would make a move to overpower this guy as he bent over to paw through the handkerchiefs, loose coins, fingernail files and paper clips. But my strong husband, always so in command, was ashen with fear as he stared at the gun now trained on his wife.

Then, inexplicably, I saw the intruder differently. He looked pitiful, his gloved hands trembling, shaking almost uncontrollably as he pawed through the drawer's contents looking for a few valuables to buy his fix. His only strength lay in a metal gun, a knife and a foul mouth.

"You will not fear the terror by night." The words read in the morning came back to me. These weren't words to Dick; they were words to me, calling me to action. "In the name of Jesus…" I surprised myself as I began to speak out in a firm, uncompromising voice: "In the name of Jesus, this is our house." Like a broken record, I repeated myself as I simultaneously took my finger and drew a clear-cut boundary between us on the carpet. I got bolder with each sentence.

Amazingly, as if pushed by an invisible force, the gunman fell over to his left side. He scrambled quickly to regain his balance and scoop up the coins. Then he hopped to his feet and in a voice like that of a little boy who had just had his hands slapped, he whimpered, "I wasn't going to hurt you." With that, he ran down the stairs and out into the night.

Dick and I fell into each other's arms and then called 911. In minutes the police were at our door, guns drawn and search dogs on leash. They scoured the property, but to this day the intruder has not been apprehended.

But I have been apprehended—by the Father's love, once more. The terror of night—and much of my lingering childhood fear of it—was routed by words of truth. And the message of Psalm 91 continues to linger on in an even more pervasive way. Had the gunman pulled the trigger and killed us, we would still be safe: The shadow of the Almighty would still have covered us. The psalmist's words are true in the morning, in the night and for eternity.

The Transformation of Ursula

From the start, it was a dangerous combination: a lunch hour with my daughter-in-law, a gourmet salad and a walk past the bookstore. The inevitable setup for one of our animated conversations about a great mutual love—our cats.

I needed a medical update on Concord, Ginny and Paul's black cat who'd been rushed three hundred miles across the mountains for surgery at Washington State University's vet school. Ginny filled me in, her face glowing with hope now that Concord was surviving his car encounter, albeit with a limp and some metal pins in one hind leg.

"Only another cat lover would understand why we go to such lengths to keep him," she explained. "Wouldn't you do the same for Felix or Ursula?"

I hedged. "Well, I'm not sure. We've had a lot of cats over the years and I have loved them all, but I guess one gets a little more philosophical about their comings and goings, especially when children come along."

Even as I said it, I hoped I hadn't dampened her unflappable determination to vote—and act—in favor of nurturing and saving life. I loved her fighting spirit. As we talked, I could see her as a mom someday, dressed in a tiger suit and battling for her kids with that same winsome tenacity.

But we weren't through with cats yet on that lunch hour. On the way back to the car, our attention was drawn to the clever display of cat books in the front window of the little bookstore. We were catapulted inside by our curiosity—two cat lovers who couldn't resist cat books. We then giggled our way through antiphonal title-reading: *Vanity Fur, The Black Cat Made Me Buy It, The Cat Who Ate Danish Modern, Cats Know Best* and *Never Take Your Cat to the Salad Bar.*

As we exited, Ginny turned and posed a challenge: "Why don't you write something about Felix and Ursula?"

Somehow Wendy, our springer spaniel, always upstaged our cats when it came to writing stories. After all, two quiet felines were hardly a match for a rambunctious, tree-climbing, counter-jumping, car-top-sitting dog. Wendy's whole lifestyle lent itself to making points about spiritual growth— forgiveness, patience, acceptance and others.

However, Ginny planted a seed that afternoon. The offshoot is a real-life anecdote about Ursula, our beautiful longhaired calico.

Ursula came to us literally from "the other side of the tracks," from a house being razed to expand one of our county dumps. My husband and daughter Jane came home from a garbage-dumping trip with her—a pitiful, whimpering lump of orange and black fur. I can still hear Jane squealing as she flew into the house, "Look, Mom, a lady gave us a free kitty."

The cat was free, of course, but also sick and filthy. Before the day was over, she'd upped her worth considerably with a trip to the vet for shots, pills and a flea bath.

Ursula, we soon realized, had more problems than being sick and dirty—she was the original 'fraidy cat. When Wendy barked, she hid behind the sofa. She shook when the dishwasher ran, hyperventilated when we vacuumed, scooted under the table when the phone rang or one of us sneezed. She was, in fact, just plain afraid of life.

A Rose for Nana

I wanted to pity Ursula, but to tell the truth, I was often annoyed and repelled by her neediness. Consequently, I ignored her much of the time and focused mainly on Felix, our drop-in cat. Felix, the consummate feline charmer. She always knew where to sit, what to do, when to move, who to brush by. Never intrusive. Subtle, attentive, clever, sensitive to our moods—all the attributes that naturally attract one to animals—or people.

Then one day, our whole cat picture changed. Ursula underwent a major transformation. Today she's a different cat. She nudges Felix at their dish; she invites herself onto the family-room sofa; she even stands her ground with Wendy over a choice morsel. In fact, she now conducts herself like a cat who knows who she is and what her life is all about. Like Pinocchio and the Velveteen Rabbit, she's become real. Seven years of being traumatized by life didn't sentence her to a lifetime of fear. She went from victim to victor.

So what happened to 'fraidy cat? Her transformation started with our kitchen remodeling. When the bulldozer and the jackhammers arrived that first day, Ursula fled to the garage. For days the house shook, the windows rattled, the noise level accelerated past anything Ursula had ever feared. She disappeared into the garage for long stretches, reappearing only for late-night forays to her food dish.

Noises terrified Ursula. If she could have read the Bible, she would have understood Job 3:25: *"What I feared has come upon me; what I dreaded has happened to me."*

One morning, with the remodeling now in full swing, she reappeared only to do an amazing, inexplicable thing: She walked right out where the builders were hammering and sawing and sat down in the midst of the construction chaos. I couldn't believe my eyes. "Ursula!" I called in my protective, rescuing voice. But she merely blinked her green eyes and smiled tolerantly at me as if I were the only one who didn't know her new secret. All day she stayed in one spot, like a feline foreman overseeing the sawdust turmoil. She didn't flinch even once at the staccato hammering over her head. No longer a 'fraidy cat, she'd become a lioness, at least inside. And more than that, she exuded an aura of contentment and peace. She was free.

I love Ursula for what she's shown us. Somehow, she chose to face her fears and step through them. And with that action, her fears lost their power to imprison her.

Jesus urges us to make that choice as well, to resist fear's paralyzing grip on our lives by acknowledging and repenting of our failure to trust Him. The Amplified Bible catches His imperative voice: *"Do not let your hearts be troubled, neither let them be afraid. [Stop allowing yourselves to be agitated and disturbed; and do not permit yourselves to be fearful and intimidated and cowardly and unsettled]"* (John 14:27).

I don't know what motivated our calico cat to make the choice that transformed her life, but I know that the Holy Spirit is at work, offering all of us empowering grace to make that same choice—to face our fears and step through them.

CHAPTER NINE

A
Touch
of
Mercy

Mercy triumphs over judgment!

James 2:13

Mercy at Midnight

I wish you could hear our neighbor Chuck tell one of his stories. You'd see his hazel eyes shine; you'd feel the compassion resonating through his rich, deep voice. Lanky, long-limbed, lover-of-the-outdoors, Chuck isn't one to parade his faith. No testimonies in which he emerges as Saint Charles. No miracles featuring himself as the hero. That's just not Chuck.

Yet after you've spent time with this struggling, transparent pilgrim, you come away refreshed. Like the Lord's hand has reached right through Chuck's heart to yours, injecting it with a gigantic shot of agape love.

Chuck's job with the university takes him around the world. His is a stressful schedule, filled with long night flights, jet lag and culture shock. But it has its pluses: time to think, time to pray, time to badger God about how his life could "really count."

Making his life count—that's Chuck's theme song. Amazingly, we never tire of hearing him play that same tune. Like a maestro addicted to great music, he loves to express his heart's passionate symphony: *How can my life be a ministry? How can I be a neighbor to those in need?*

Recently, Chuck was barbecuing oysters for us at their beach place on Puget Sound. He struck up the familiar music: "With all the overseas trips I've taken, with all the poverty and sickness I've seen, I'm convinced the Lord wants me to help the hurting. But I'm overwhelmed with the magnitude of it all. How can we know what He really wants us to do? What can we do that would make a difference for the Kingdom?"

His wife grinned, shook her head and rolled her eyes. "Honey, why don't you stop asking questions and tell the Greenwoods what happened here last Sunday night?"

So while the tide eased in across the sand and the noisy gulls glided over the water, Chuck told us his adventure from the previous weekend:

"Paul, our neighbor, and I were sitting right out here on the beach poking the bonfire, waiting for it to die out. It was late, close to midnight, and Barb had already gone into the cabin for the night. The water was unusually still. Without a moon, it was pitch black. We started talking about how we could serve people in a way that could make a difference. Could God use us to help people in a significant way? How?

"We were tossing around a lot of ideas, trying to get a fix on what avenues of service would be open to us, given our ages and circumstances. Both of us were aware of noises out on the sound, but that's not unusual for Sunday night. The channel is often filled with boaters heading in after a weekend, partying all the way back to Seattle. We never gave it a second thought.

"But during a gap in our conversation, I thought I heard someone yelling. We walked to the water's edge and listened again. 'Someone's calling for help,' I told Paul. 'Can't you hear it? We'd better get the boat and check this out.'

"Paul didn't hear a thing. In fact, he warned me, 'Chuck, it's too dark out there. No way should we head out in your little ten-foot Livingston. We need more than a nine-horse motor—we need a spotlight and a bigger boat.'

"I was more sure by the minute: Someone *was* calling for help. I couldn't risk waking up in the morning and finding a body washed ashore in front of our cabin because I hadn't made any effort to help. I had to try. I told Paul I was heading out, even if I had to go alone. But I didn't. Paul pulled the boat into the water while I grabbed a flashlight and a rope from the house.

"We moved out in the direction of the noises, zigzagging our way through the darkness. It was like looking for the proverbial needle in the haystack. We'd shut off the motor, listen to determine the direction of the cries for help, then start up again, going toward the voices. They'd yell, 'Help!' and we'd yell back, 'We're coming, we're coming!'

"Finally we connected: Two men, one a big two-hundred-sixty-pounder, the other a little guy, were clinging to their swamped kayak. Within seconds of our spotting them, the little guy doubled over in a fetal position, and passed out from hypothermia.

"I can't tell you how we rescued these guys. Another neighbor came alongside in his boat; but even so, the logistics were impossible. You just don't haul a two-hundred-sixty-pound, six-foot-five-inch guy over the bow of a little dinghy—not unless maybe there are a few angels around boosting him in and steadying the boat."

Chuck finished telling us his story—how they called the medics, showered the men, rubbed them down and put them in warm sleeping bags while waiting for the aid car. Two lives saved. Not on the dusty road from Jericho to Jerusalem, but on the waters of Puget Sound. Two men rescued. Not by those who passed by on "the other side." Not by those with all the answers on what constitutes ministry. But by those whose hearts beat with the Father's love. Those open and available. Those who have mercy.

I don't worry about Chuck's finding ways to serve the Lord. He's got the Good Samaritan story past his head and emblazoned on his heart. He's caught the point of the parable: We serve God—*right where we are*—when we act with the same mercy we've first received from Him.

It's through lives like Chuck's that I clearly hear Jesus' words to me: "Go and do likewise."

Surprised by Mercy

reacherous Turn and Harrowing Hill—sounds like a couple of allegorical streets out of *Pilgrim's Progress*, doesn't it? But they're not. They're simply homegrown names for a hilly section of road in our suburban Seattle neighborhood—a stretch that has become notorious for its accident record.

Rarely referred to by its proper name, Carlyle Hall Road, this particular piece of road has had a distressing number of accidents, including several fatalities. One of the most tragic involved three teenagers coming home from the beach one afternoon. The driver, forgetting to slow down at the top of the hill, failed to negotiate the curve and the car flipped over in midair, landing upside down in someone's front yard. Two kids were killed.

Since then the police have responded to the neighbors' pleas to patrol the area and enforce the twenty-five-mile-an-hour speed limit.

I drive that stretch several times a week, and I was thrilled that police were attempting to halt the excessive speeding. Although the speed limit is conspicuously posted in several spots, it's easy to forget to slow down from the previous thirty-five-mile-per-hour zone.

Then one night, hurrying home from a late meeting at

Carol Greenwood

church, I saw the flashing blue light of a patrol car at the foot of the hill. *Good enough,* I mused. *The only way speeders are going to learn is if they get stopped and have to pay the penalty for their negligence.*

I automatically braked down the hill, passed the patrol car and eased to a stop at the intersection. I couldn't resist glancing in my rearview mirror to spy on the scenario I imagined—the patrolman writing out a ticket and making his point about safe driving to some speeder. Instead, I saw the flashing blue light advancing behind *my* car, edging *me* to the shoulder.

Wonder if my taillight is burned out, I thought as I rolled down my window, ready to hear about my car's problem. The problem, I soon discovered, was not with my car, but with me.

"In a hurry?" queried the young officer. "My partner's up at the straight stretch where twenty-five-miles-an-hour is posted, and his radar clocked you at thirty-eight. By the time you reached me you were at thirty-two."

"Me?" I answered incredulously. "I'm just on my way home from church." My face flushed at my self-righteous dodge.

"Driver's license, please." The officer was all business. He took my license, strode back to his car and checked my driving record and our car license on his computer.

Five minutes passed, but it seemed like fifteen. My thoughts began racing to my defense. He's young enough to be my son. I wonder if this is his first week out and he's overzealous to bring in some kind of quota on traffic tickets. I waited with my eyes glued to my rearview mirror, consoling myself that my good driving record would get me off with a warning this time.

Returning to my window, the officer handed back my

license. "Did you know that two teenagers were killed on this road a few months ago?"

"Yes. Our son was on the track team with them. It was a terrible loss."

"We're concerned about saving lives on this stretch and we're not compromising our standards, even for good drivers. You have a choice to either mail in a check for fifty-seven dollars or go before the judge if you want to protest it."

Two weeks later I drove to the district court for my late-afternoon hearing before the judge.

"Well, well, caught going down the old Treacherous Turn, eh?" The judge, in his early fifties, was kindly and relaxed. "Your address tells me that you live in the neighborhood. Probably just slipped this time. However, one slip could be just as lethal as those of the habitual speeder."

He was right and I knew it. My flimsy rationalization didn't excuse me: I was guilty. I reached for my checkbook, but the judge intervened.

"We're determined to whip this area into a safe stretch by enforcing the law there. I can't compromise that decision. The only thing I can do is give you something you don't deserve—I'll drop the fine in half." He looked me directly in the eye and added, "Let's just call it *mercy*."

Mercy? I couldn't believe it! In the judge's chambers of that little district traffic court where I deserved punishment, I was given mercy. The proud, self-righteous one, guilty of breaking the law, had met up with an honest judge who wouldn't compromise his high standards of justice. Yet he had given compassion to the undeserving offender.

As I drove home that day, I remembered anew that justice and mercy comprise the heart of the Gospel. A just and merciful God has reached down to save us. We don't have to spend time in flimsy rationalization because the Judge is on our side! He has already paid for all our slips, foibles, mistakes and sins through the sacrifice of His own Son. Let us share that same life-changing Gospel. In a world riddled with "treacherous turns" and "harrowing hills," this is really Good News.

CHAPTER TEN

A
Touch
of
Hope

*"For I know the plans I have for you," declares
the* Lord, *"plans to prosper you and not to harm
you, plans to give you hope and a future."*
Jeremiah 29:11

$\mathcal{A}$ntidote for the "$\mathcal{O}$verwhelms"

$\mathcal{P}$eter, Jacob, Gretchen and Frieda. Four little basket-carrying Dutch kids. Remember them from your childhood reading? Innocence bundled in excitement, they were out for a day gathering nuts in the country. A magnificent day. In fact, they were so successful, their baskets soon overflowed with their cache. Finally, toward evening, still exuberant, they skipped home under darkening skies.

All except Peter. The folktale tells us that he spied water soaking into the sand along the dike and he stopped. "The water—the water from the sea is pouring through a hole in the dike." None of the other children felt Peter's urgency or perceived his worry. But he was adamant. He knew it was only a matter of time before the brewing storm would push the sea through the ever-widening hole and rush in to flood the land. As the others scurried home in the descending twilight, Peter turned back to the dike.

We know the rest. The single-minded, brave little Dutch boy thrust his arm into the hole in the wall. All night he stayed, shivering and trembling, as the bitterly cold waters of the North Sea pummeled the dike with its human plug.

When morning comes, Peter is rescued, the dike repaired and the flood averted. For a finale, a squad of soldiers carries the young hero home on their shoulders to his frantic mother.

I've thought of this little story lately when Christians tell me they feel overwhelmed. Tired. Stressed out. Pulled in every direction.

Fearful of living in the world of the twenty-first century. Weary of coping in a society where the pace of living is accelerating exponentially.

Know the feeling? I do. You're coasting along in your own little world, listening to praise tapes in your car, reading the Bible through in a year, praying for your kids, picking up litter on the sidewalks—doing the "good Christian" things; and then, out of the blue, the "overwhelms" hit. Like an attack dog, they go for the throat.

Child abuse, drugs, school shootings—the news bombards you and emotionally wrestles you to the ground. When you stagger to your feet, you feel clobbered. Here you are, minding your own business, when some kind of cosmic garbage truck stops at your place—and dumps. The onslaught hits. The world is not only spinning too fast, it is not user-friendly. Evil seems rampant—and mutating.

When the "overwhelms" hit, my first reaction is to run. And the second is like Peter's—I'll thrust myself against this onslaught. I'll plug the hole so the dike won't break. Urgency can be a clever distorter of truth. And, in its grip, I forget who's responsible for this planet and its people. From there I spiral downward.

Are there antidotes for this kind of poisonous thinking? Yes! At a recent family dinner our kids reminded me of one: laughter. Time and again it has gotten our family back on track. Laughter. Unbridled, spontaneous, belly-level, roll-on-the-floor laughter.

"Remember the trip to Yellowstone?" The four of them—now all young adults—posed the question in unison as they

A Rose for Nana

sat reminiscing around our table, recalling the day laughter rescued the whole family. Picture the scene:

The perfect American family returning home from a two-week "dream" vacation—exploring a national park. Four kids packed into a station wagon with sleeping bags, suitcases and the ice chest. Never forget the ice chest. We used it to separate two girls who were pinching each other with mortal intent.

Everyone was tired. I'd thrown my back out. Dick was worn down with justifying why "every schoolchild should see and *appreciate* his country." In cryptic language, the kids took turns expressing why they wished they'd been born into another family, one that toured Hawaii or Disneyland.

We felt like the American Gothic couple: silent and uptight. The kids were fighting and we were mad. We hurtled past the Craters of the Moon in southern Idaho with nary a mention of its geological uniqueness. We exchanged a silent, but knowing, message: *Our car is full of ungrateful beasties.*

Then I sneezed—loud enough to wake the dead. A snicker arose from a kid in the second seat. I started giggling. Timidly. Then real laughter erupted and spread like brushfire. We were all laughing our heads off. Dick pulled into a rest stop and the six of us piled out, trying to walk while doubled over in hysterical laughter. We walked to our respective restrooms laughing, and we emerged still laughing.

Onlookers shook their heads. One man made an aside to his wife: "Weird family." She responded, "Catch the license plate." That set us off for another ten miles of hilarious, unrestrained laughter. And then, a new perspective. Relief. Peace. And even harmony again.

Long before Norman Cousins laughed himself back to health by watching funny movies or anyone ever heard of laughter releasing healing endorphins, the Bible advocated it. Ecclesiastes reminds us of a *"season for every activity under*

151

Carol Greenwood

heaven...a time to weep and a time to laugh" (Ecclesiastes 3:1 and 4).

The Holy Spirit is well able to show us how to "plug the holes" when the tide of evil pounds against the dikes around us. But oh, how we need to take our God much more seriously and ourselves much less so. And Christians, we, of all people, can afford to laugh. Not at the tragedy of sin and all its fallout. But because God is still in charge and because He has the final word, we need to laugh—especially in the midst of the "overwhelms."

Penetrate the Darkness

"We're heading for the island!" The kids could hardly contain their excitement. It was an Easter-week vacation, and a friend and I decided to combine our broods and take our collective eight children for a few days' break in the San Juan Islands, north of Seattle.

Our husbands, whose schedules were busiest in mid-April, commended us for our bravery and promised us their prayers.

So two aging station wagons, loaded down with sleeping bags, groceries, games and two moms with four kids each, drove onto the super ferry at Anacortes for the trip through the beautiful San Juan archipelago to Orcas Island.

Our stay was filled with simple fun: beachcombing, excursions in the rowboat out to Freeman's Island, trips to the town's craft shop during rainstorms, games and the ritual evening marshmallow roasts. Sure, a few minor squabbles erupted between siblings, but overall, the kids were congenial, content to just have fun.

On our last night, the youngest in our group, Kristi, got sick. Nothing serious—just a stomach bug or a mild overdose of goodies. But since the upset came at 10:30 p.m., I volunteered to fetch the clean linens while her mother comforted her. No heroic errand on my part, just a ten-minute stroll down the tree-lined road to the manager's office. I arrived in a flash, explained my mission, collected the fresh linens and turned to retrace my steps.

When I was about a quarter of the way back to the cabin, the large vapor lamp illuminating the road clicked off—totally without warning. I stopped in my tracks. I blinked. I squinted and tried to refocus. I lowered my gaze toward the ground, as if looking for those track lights lining the sides of an airplane aisle—the ones on the floor designed to light up in an emergency. But there were no little lights here.

The thick branches of the towering Douglas firs and a moonless, cloudy sky together had formed a veritable black blanket over that road. I understood the situation, but even that knowledge didn't shed any real light where I needed it. While I was certainly in no danger of falling into the water or off a precipice, it was simply too dark to see anything, much less navigate down the road. *This is ridiculous. Why didn't I bring a flashlight?* Finally, more amused than anxious, I faced my options: stay put until someone comes searching for me or get down on my knees and crawl. I chose to crawl.

As a hiker, there were many times when I'd needed an extra sweater or another energy bar. But I was neither cold nor hungry now. My problem was the darkness, and my need was to penetrate it. I needed help. A flashlight. A lighted match. I'd even have settled for taking the hand of someone who could have led me safely through the dark.

Persistence, punctuated by chuckles over the humor of the situation, ultimately propelled me forward on my knees and to the cabin door. Once securely back, I dove into the linen-changing project and gave little thought to the darkness and my great need for a light. However, nearly a year later, while I was reading the Sermon on the Mount in Matthew, my memory did a flashback.

A Rose for Nana

Like instant replay, I was back crawling along that Orcas Island dirt road, groping my way through the impenetrable darkness. This time I didn't giggle. I was confronted by the truth of Jesus' simple commission: *"You are the light of the world. A city on a hill cannot be hidden. Neither do people light a lamp and put it under a bowl. Instead they put it on its stand, and it gives light to everyone in the house. In the same way, let your light shine"* (Matthew 5:14-16).

"Penetrate the darkness," Jesus seemed to say. "As a candle is lit by fire, so your life is ignited by Mine. That light has the capacity to illuminate your path, to pierce the darkness, to dispel shadows, to expose evil and to resist the work of the usurper." Jesus knew that the only power in the universe capable of transforming darkness into light is God's life. *In him was life, and that life was the light of men* (John 1:4).

As His light bearers, we are called to be determined, committed people who fight passivity, hand-wringing and complaining in our encounters with the wicked forces of darkness—forces that wreak havoc in our homes, churches and nations. Like the virtuous woman of Proverbs 31, we are challenged to *"get up while it is still dark"* and not to let our candles go out *at night*, to pray, to intercede, to persevere in works of kindness initiated by the Spirit, to lay down our lives for others in the midst of what appears to be the very darkest and most hopeless of hours.

Dark is dark, I learned while crawling on that dirt road with my bundle of sheets and towels. We need not waste our time analyzing the darkness, for God presses us to move forward, even in the dark, to carry on the work of His Kingdom. We can be encouraged by His call to action and the promise of His empowering presence: *"Arise, shine, for your light has come, and the glory of the LORD rises upon you"* (Isaiah 60:1).

Carol Greenwood

In the midst of a crooked and depraved generation, we are to shine as stars in the universe, holding out the word of life (see Philippians 2:15-16) with the full knowledge that His light shines in darkness and darkness has never overcome it (see John 1:5).

Rx for Sinking Spells

One day last week I crumpled. Caved in. Folded my tent. Without a doubt, I had a full-blown case of "the staggers." You wouldn't have missed it if you'd seen me drive home from work on "limp," drag myself through the front door and drop into the rocking chair in the kitchen.

"Enough, world," I said as I leaned over to bump the phone off its hook. I let out a granddaddy sigh, then switched to groan as I heard the evening paper hit our front porch. And instead of bringing it in, I just kicked off my shoes and growled at our springer spaniel. *Well, why not?* I thought. *In this dog-eat-dog world, we deserve a little role reversal once in a while.*

Stunned, Wendy slunk outside and quickly passed along the word to our cats, Felix and Ursula: *Beware, baaad mood inside.*

At our house, we've always called such downers "sinking spells." These are times when you feel that life has wrestled you to the mat or that you've just pushed the down button of your personal elevator and expressed yourself to the subbasement. Paraphrasing the words of the poet Wordsworth, "The world is too much with you."

157

Carol Greenwood

Usually, at least for me, what we're really talking about is perspective—losing it—and then wallowing in its void.

It's rarely the big crises that steal our vision. More often it's little things piling up that fuel a "sinking spell." The Bible calls them "the little foxes that ruin a vineyard."

That day last week, I could almost hear those little foxes barking. An ugly tale of child abuse spilled out on the morning news; a friend called, anguishing over her mother's struggle with Alzheimer's disease; a college friend despaired for her alcoholic husband; another friend cried on the phone as she described the ridicule she'd gotten for refusing sex before marriage. Like a live target, I felt pain shooting from every quarter—physical, emotional, spiritual. Was there no end to it? I rallied to brew some tea, then sank again while the tea steeped. "Oh, God," I moaned, "there's too much pain in the world. I hurt."

Where do you go when you double over with that kind of pain? I wanted to put life on hold and escape to Shangri-la. Instead, I went upstairs; pulled on my jeans, sweatshirt and tennis shoes; grabbed my garden gloves and pruning shears; and headed for the backyard.

The "little foxes" weren't barking outside. Or at least I couldn't hear them as I squared off against the blackberry vines invading our property. Forgetting all about the problems of the world, I yanked, pulled and slashed at the entangled network of roots for two solid hours.

Then it surfaced—quietly, gently—perhaps like the still small voice Elijah heard. Unmistakable words: "Carol, it's okay to hurt."

Had I heard right? "It's okay to hurt"—the words delivered too much comfort to dismiss idly. For a few days I carried them around, mulling over their impact. And then a friend told me about her weekend with her ten-year-old son.

Grant, she'd felt, needed to see more of life than he was experiencing in the comfortable suburb where they lived. Mom took son in tow, and they spent a Sunday afternoon observing the street people in downtown Seattle.

For several hours they walked the street. Grant stared at the people in food lines, witnessed the despair in their faces, noted their worn-out shoes, smelled the urine and garbage. To his surprise, these weren't faceless "bums" lying around drunk in the back alleys of the city. Unemployed and homeless, these were real people—young, middle-aged and old. Families with little kids—cute little kids.

After a while, Grant stopped talking. In fact, neither one spoke as they drove back to their suburb. Then, without warning, in the middle of the freeway, Grant's voice pierced the silence. "Mom," he wailed, "I can feel it coming." He gasped for breath and let the tidal wave hit. "It's *heartbrokenness*," he sobbed, giving vent as best he could to what his tender eyes and ears had taken in.

Heartbrokenness, sinking spell, whatever term we use, if you've experienced it, you know it. And what is more, you're in good company. In his book *Inside Out*, Larry Crabb describes this feeling as a "core sadness that will not go away—evidence of honest living in a sad world." Jesus knew this pain intimately.

According to Dr. Crabb, "no matter how richly we experience the Lord, we cannot avoid the impact of living in a fallen world as a fallen being. Neither could our Lord. In perfect communion with the Father, yet He was still a man of sorrows, gripped to the point of tears by the hardness of men's hearts."

We may never physically stand and weep over Jerusalem as Jesus did. But we can let our heartbrokenness, our sinking spells, drive us to face our pain for what it is—the sign of utter hopelessness in a world adrift from God. And then we can make another choice: to let that pain drive us passionately to His perspective—and His arms.

Two Little Words for Moms

his one's for you, moms. Or, if you're English, "mums." Daughters, listen up: You'll be encouraged too.

My credentials for your attention? My authority? As mother of four and grandmother of nine, I'm ready, finally, to confidently pass on some of my hard-learned secrets of motherhood.

I'm not a knitter or even a quilter. So when my eldest daughter, Anne, was pregnant with our first grandchild, I began fretting. Without these skills, maybe I didn't have the "stuff" to become a bona-fide, picture-carrying granny. Maybe things had changed so much since my diapering days that my old techniques for burping and patting would fuel, not soothe, gassy tummies. This stack of *maybe*'s ultimately catapulted me into a familiar heap at the throne of grace where, in my Moses-falsetto voice, I squeaked out all my inadequacies.

The Lord, of course, recognized my voice, yet He didn't buy my complaining. Instead, He countered with His grace—again. Tough, no-nonsense grace, the measure of which spurred me back on track with a nudge and a commission. This time it was simple: "Pass on what you've learned."

So bear with me. I'm feeling like the Titus woman, that it is now time to hand down to my daughter—and to you as well—the two best insights I acquired in the crucible of motherhood (see Titus 2:4).

Like my friends, I read all sorts of childrearing books. I took classes at church and preschools, gleaned from my friends, treasured my husband's counsel and prayed. Yet nothing prepared me for the trauma of toe-to-toe skirmishes with a teenager.

We've had four red-blooded kids go through this stage of life—and each one at some point brought me banging on Heaven's door for help. But one day stands out above all the rest. The Red Sea parted that day, and while the wilderness ahead still held daily challenges, my motherhood badge was stamped "Delivered" from then on.

The day dawned sunny and clear. Perfect Seattle weather. Perfect day for Paul, our easygoing fourteen-year-old, to mow the back lawn, a simple morning project. However, as it dragged on, I was aware that he stopped the mower more than usual and kept popping in to take calls on the upstairs phone. I thought nothing of it, except to note the grass clippings piling up on the stairs.

"Hey, Mom," he whistled on his way back from the fifth or sixth phone call. "Here's a permission slip for you to sign. I need your signature by Monday."

"Sure. What's it for?" I asked routinely, reaching to sign it without my glasses.

"Oh, nothing important. One of the school's little forms. Just put your John Hancock on the line. You can do it without your glasses."

Instinctively, I grabbed my glasses and started to read the document in Paul's hand.

"No big deal, Mom. I just need your okay for my locker partner choice for next year. Here's a pen. Sign away."

Face eager, he fairly panted, but his eyes evaded mine. I looked at him, then at the grass clippings on the stairs and signaled for time-out to finish reading the little yellow slip.

"Paul, you put down Linda's name for your locker partner. Why don't you go with Tom or Brad? Are you sure you want a girl for a locker partner? You may not feel the same way by next spring."

Sound motherly counsel, but Paul didn't like it. He bounded upstairs to the phone; I could hear his anguish from downstairs. Still, the more I thought about it, the "righter" I became. Suddenly we were locked in controversy.

"Mom, you've really upset Linda! She's throwing up. She thinks you hate her. Do you want to ruin our year?"

"I like you both," I protested, "but over the long haul, I don't think this is a wise decision."

That did it. We were in combat. Charges and counter-charges. We weren't tangling over a big moral question; I couldn't comprehend Paul's reaction, but we were in deep. This was war—artillery and cannons. And I was the target. "Worst mother in the school. Old-fashioned. Stubborn. Heartless."

Inside, I was crumbling. Caving in. Ready to weaken and sign the silly card. "God," I groaned, "You picked the wrong woman to be a mother. Four kids and I've just struck out. I'm not qualified for this job; I don't have what it takes for motherhood." I snorted and moaned as I held court with my complaints.

Then, while I was absentmindedly admiring the roses against the backdrop of the blue sky, two little words punctured my pity party: *love and perspective.* How simple! So like the Lord to meet me in my emptiness and build me up, bringing hope. Of course He equips moms!

First, *love*—His for us. Redemptive and unconditional. And when received again and again, we become equipped to make tough decisions, to love despite rebuff, to hang in when the shots fly, to look discouragement in the face and choose to love back.

And second, *perspective*—that God-given, long-haul view that comes with experience and maturity. We can love and train because we see the bigger picture of life. We know how much our kids need tough love, acceptance and discipline to carry them through this broken world. We don't have to capitulate to the NOW.

Love and perspective. Two little words that also remind us of our Father's care for us. Hang on to them, moms. And hang on to Him.

CHAPTER ELEVEN

A
Touch
at
Christmas

"Arise, shine, for your light has come,
and the glory of the LORD rises upon you."

Isaiah 60:1

The Length of Love

One year Dick and I decided to celebrate our wedding anniversary at the ocean. Unusual for us because we're so attached to Puget Sound, where we live. Its inlets, its gentle tides, its extraordinary sea life and its rocky beaches surrounded by evergreen trees have satisfied us over the years in ways that defy explanation. However, this spring, we yearned to see the Pacific Ocean, to be awed by a force bigger than ourselves.

And we were not disappointed. We walked along the shore in front of the lodge where we stayed. The pounding surf thundered against the sandy beach, loud and unrelenting. Magnificent, but at the same time almost frightening. Both of us made a stab at describing how we felt, but finally we simply stopped talking. All the usual adjectives stuck in our throats. Dwarfed by power and majesty, we were silenced by the ocean's grandeur and our insignificance.

We ate dinner that night at a little pizza place a few blocks back from the crashing waves. "I'm not sure I can cope with just sticking around the ocean," Dick volunteered. "How about heading inland tomorrow? Maybe explore some of the bays and villages on the other side of the peninsula?"

"You've got my vote, Honey," I assured him. "I'm feeling

intimidated by all that water. Out of my comfort zone against such bigness. I think I'll have to take the ocean in smaller doses."

That's how we happened to stumble upon the little village of Nahcotta along Willapa Bay. Little more than a wide spot in the road, Nahcotta was in the throes of its biggest event of the year—a garlic festival. We couldn't believe our eyes. Hordes of people, locals and tourists, descended on a narrow strip of road where dozens of booths proudly extolled the marvels of garlic.

There were garlic bouquets, garlic presses, garlic wreaths, garlic cookbooks, as well as every imaginable culinary goody—soup, salad, pasta and bread. Dick and I capitulated to the enticing aroma of Hungarian sausage soup. Then, foolishly, we capped off our lunch with a frosted raspberry torte, never dreaming it too was laced with garlic.

But the pièce de résistance wasn't among all the garlic-laden food. Instead, it was in the afternoon's major attraction: an outdoor garlic wedding. We had no idea this was an annual event, one where more than seven hundred couples had applied to be married. And here we were, celebrating our anniversary and finding ourselves unintentionally among the wedding guests.

The milling crowd squeezed us into the front row, next to the arch where the bride and groom would exchange their vows. Talk about a switch from the day before! From two insignificant beach walkers we'd just been upgraded to honored-guests status. We were directed to a roped-off area where we rubbed elbows with the TV crews and photojournalists who'd driven down from Seattle to report the garlic wedding.

Enter bridal attendants: two women dressed as garlic cloves in puffy green and white pads, with white tights and pink slippers. They were followed down the aisle by another woman dressed as an oversized crab, complete with orange shell and pinchers.

As the marimba and the bongo drums played under the canopy behind the arch, the groom, his best man and the black-gowned judge slipped under the ropes and took their places facing the crowd.

Dick nudged me, "Look to your right, or you'll miss the bride." I didn't want to miss anything, although I admit my curiosity was edging toward skepticism.

Enter the bride and maid of honor. Dressed in gray tuxes, they were seated on top of a white convertible that quietly nosed its way through the crowd and stopped short of the lattice arch. They hopped off and strolled down the gravel aisle.

The judge made a few opening remarks to the crowd, and the ceremony began. The carnival-type atmosphere suddenly felt empty. "Something's missing," I whispered to Dick.

"You mean *Someone*," he whispered back.

The judge asked the bride and groom to repeat their vows after him: "For better, for worse; for richer, for poorer; in sickness and in health." He paused. Then he delivered the clincher: "As long as love lasts."

As long as love lasts! The words hit us like cold water in the face.

How long does human love last? What is the length of it? Dick and I couldn't speak for the garlic couple, yet we knew from our own experience that our love was at times stretched, strained and battered until it was threadbare under the stress of daily living. Job pressures, financial strains, time demands with four kids, not to mention our own penchant for selfishness, all extracted from love's store. There were times when we felt like we'd "given at the office" or at home all day and had no love left to give.

When Jesus comes to weddings, miracles have been known to happen. Had it not been that He took the water of our frail humanity in His hands and turned it into fine wine, we never

169

would have known the secret of rich, staying love: *the Father's unconditional, everlasting love undergirding our own. Supplying over and over again what we lacked.*

At Christmas we look again at this kind of love and try to comprehend it in the infant Jesus. He's so unlike the awesome things that intimidate us—like pounding, crashing oceans. He is also unlike the world's hollow counterfeits. We can hardly take Him in—absolute power and strength clothed in weakness, helplessness and vulnerability—and destined to die for us.

How long does God's love last? Forever! What is the length of it? Measure it in Jesus!

Great Expectations

The Lumpy-Clam-Chowder Story has become one of our family's favorite Christmas stories. While we usually prefer telling the funny reruns from past Christmases, the chowder story has, nevertheless, become a family classic. Over the years this tale continues to warm our hearts in much the same way a hearty homemade soup warms our bodies on a wintry night.

It happened on Christmas Eve. Our house was fully decorated, fragrant with the scents we were accustomed to as part of our annual festivities—a mountain-fresh Douglas fir tree, pine boughs, a variety of food aromas lingering from the morning's baking, the fragrance of vanilla candles and, last but not least, the smell of clam chowder simmering on the stove, the traditional main dish for our light Christmas Eve supper.

I added the finishing touches to the chowder, fried bits of bacon and chopped parsley. *Hmmm, smells pretty good,* I thought. *Almost ready to serve.* The phone rang. Within ten minutes I'd received three phone calls, all from people we'd invited to dinner the next day. For one reason or another, they were calling to cancel. They couldn't make it for Christmas dinner.

The last call was the most difficult for me. Dad, at the last minute, felt he just wasn't up to the six-hour drive across the snowy Cascade Mountains from his house to ours. Assuring us he'd miss us, he concluded our conversation with the promise he'd make it "next year for sure."

I was mildly annoyed. After all, we'd made a lot of special preparations with each of these people in mind. The kids had decorated place cards for everyone, and we'd even doubled the recipes on some of the salads—"just for them."

Annoyance turned to irritation. This was really short notice to give a hostess—especially at Christmastime. Disappointment moved in fast.

I loved having the house filled with friends on Christmas. I had expected all these extra people to be with us, to enjoy the holiday together, to enhance our family celebration—and now, in ten minutes, my expectations had all been smashed.

Paul, our son, who was ten at the time, came into the kitchen to check on the progress of supper and immediately ran headlong into the gloomy cloud hovering over my preparations. I stood at the stove staring into the chowder. Paul edged close to my side.

Without a word he handed me the wooden spoon. Not wanting to be critical, and at the same time sensitive to my unfestive mood, he spoke hesitantly, "Mom, lumps are in the chowder. And I don't think they're clams."

Sure enough, big lumps had formed while I'd been talking on the phone.

"Lumps could ruin the clam chowder, Mom." Wisdom again, from a ten-year-old. "We've got to smash those lumps and save the soup."

The lumps in the chowder were nothing compared to the one in my throat. Yet Paul was suggesting we could turn things around, and, in my dark hour, I needed to hear that.

Things did turn around. That very night. First we tackled the lumps in the clam chowder with the adept handling of two wooden spoons. Together Paul and I attacked those big, white intruders and systematically pressed them against the bottom of the pot, squashing them one by one.

Then I went to work on the lump in my throat.

That took more than the press of the wooden spoon. Some of my cherished ideas of what *had* to happen at Christmas—my misplaced expectations—needed to be "squashed" as vigorously as the lumps in the chowder.

As soon as I'd made that choice, an idea popped into my head. I would place three phone calls—one to a friend, one to my aunt and one back to Dad. Each person, surprised by the unexpected Christmas Eve phone call, heard from me for the first time how deeply their love and kindnesses through the years had enriched my life. I reminded them of specific things they'd said or done. I heard the voices on the other end of the line warm with surprise and joy as I told them how much I cared about them.

Unbeknown to us then, all three of these precious people would not live to celebrate another Christmas on earth. Our young pastor friend, at twenty-six, died two weeks later of a ruptured aneurysm. My dad died of a heart attack and my aunt of a stroke—both within six months.

We believe our Christmas Eve "turnaround" was the Lord's grace to us—a special gift that has changed every Christmas since. It started when we saw that a sturdy wooden spoon and some determination could salvage a lumpy chowder. Then we focused on the center of our Christmas celebration—Jesus, the Babe of Bethlehem—the One who not only "saved the day" by giving grace to rout my disappointment and misplaced expectations, but also who continues to "save us from ourselves" every day.

Carol Greenwood

No circumstance can sidetrack the marvel of this gift. An unspeakable gift—the gift of Jesus, the Savior of the world and our Savior. Truly we can say, *"My hope and expectation are from Him"* (Psalm 62:5, AMP).

Hiccup in the Cathedral

If you've visited the city of York in Northern England, you're not likely to forget its magnificent cathedral, the York Minster. When my husband and I stepped inside this enormous church—the largest Gothic cathedral in England—we instinctively stopped talking. And walking. For a few minutes we stood motionless in the nave, transfixed by the size and antiquity of this place.

As curious, excited tourists, we had no idea how dwarfed and insignificant we'd feel in this massive structure, and, at the same time, how captivated we'd be by its beauty. We finally "came to" and followed the guide to the altar where the late afternoon sun streamed through the medieval stained-glass windows, splashed over our faces and danced across our tennis shoes. Again, we were speechless.

A few years ago, we were back in York with two daughters and a friend. "You're on your own for seeing York," Dick announced, "except for one mandatory first stop—the Minster."

We arrived at the cathedral by 3:59 p.m., one minute before evensong began. The usher reluctantly raised the restraining rope and let the five of us in, cautioning us to tiptoe across the stone floor. The woman on my right turned and frowned. The man behind me cleared his throat. I cringed at the obvious chastisement for irreverent tardiness.

The choir director raised his hands, and in that infinitesimal moment before the first note sounded the little girl next to me hiccuped—loudly. Then twice more—just as loudly.

"Mummy," she gasped, "I hiccuped." Her face was red. Mummy's face was redder. Everyone in that packed cathedral—the rector, the choir director, the choir and the congregation heard the clear echo of a child's hiccup resonating through the infallible acoustics of a church built in 1220. But only our family heard her plaintive sob as she buried her head in her mother's shoulder: "Mummy, did I scare God away?"

Can you identify with her cry? I can. How often Satan has foisted that lie across our planet: that somehow our behavior—or even just our humanness—scares off a capricious God at the slightest provocation. Usually when we need Him the most.

Once we buy that deception, we're ripe for the enemy's next ploy—to scare us into believing our worst fear: that we're really alone in this world after all.

If you're like me, at times in your life you've felt like an abandoned orphan, as if God were off hosting a party, but He'd forgotten to mail your invitation. You wondered if you'd "hiccuped" once too often, and He finally threw in the towel with you. After all, He'd put up with you long enough and He had the cosmos to take care of.

No wonder we enjoy Christmas so much! What a perfect time to combat those lies with the truth—the truth that we have a God who runs *to* us, not *from* us—the truth about a loving Father who demonstrated His approachability two thousand years ago when He sent His love packaged in a helpless babe—the truth of Jesus who can be known by faith as One who seeks to rescue us, not abandon us.

A Rose for Nana

Hearts are unusually open and soft at Christmas. It can be a wonderful time for renewal—for ourselves and for those around us. A time to retell the arsenal of stories from the Bible (and from experiences) that remind us again that God is always with us.

Remember Simeon? He was a mere bit player in the nativity drama, but we can relate to him as we think of his soul's longing to see the promised Messiah. God finally gave him "hands-on" knowledge of the Lord. Simeon took the infant Jesus in his arms and declared, *"My eyes have seen your salvation, which you have prepared in the sight of all people"* (Luke 2:30,31).

And Anna the prophetess. She prayed and fasted in the Temple every day. At age eighty-four, she saw the answer to her prayers as she witnessed Simeon's blessing on Jesus, the Hope of Israel. She knew God's promise was true. Both saints lived to see the evidence that God does not leave His people. They saw Emmanuel!

A dear retired Estonian pastor friend of ours tells of his most memorable Christmas—when the Lord made Himself known in the barracks of a freezing Siberian prison camp during World War II.

The men had secretly dragged in a tiny fir tree from the woods where they labored ten hours a day. They decorated it with scraps of paper and medicine vials they had saved to fill with heating oil. When they lit the oil and sang a Christmas hymn, those weary men, stripped of home, family and traditions, experienced the presence of their Savior. Jesus was with them, strengthening their weak bodies and encouraging their spirits.

In her book *Life and Death in Shanghai*, Nien Cheng, a courageous Chinese woman imprisoned for seven years during the Cultural Revolution of the 1960s, describes a Christmas Eve in her cramped, dank cell. Physically and emotionally

Carol Greenwood

depleted from hours of interrogation and abuse and engulfed in aloneness, she suddenly heard the Father speak. From two cells down, a lovely lyric soprano voice dared to penetrate that evil atmosphere with "Silent Night"—on pitch and in perfect Chinese. Emmanuel was with her!

At Christmas, we're tempted to rail against those things that appear to keep the Lord at a distance—the noisy malls, the blatant commercialism, the selfish materialism, all our "hiccups in the cathedral."

How much better to do what the angels did when Jesus was born in Bethlehem—Rejoice! Like the angels, let us sing it out for all the world to hear—"Glory to God in the highest."

Walking for Life

I read something in a national newsmagazine that confirmed one of my cherished contentions: A daily walk makes a difference in one's marriage. I knew it! I'd never seen it in print before, but there, between a foreign policy report and an economic forecast, was a full-page article extolling the merits of a nightly stroll with one's spouse.

I was impressed. Not just because of my prejudice for walking, but because the author had done his homework. Although he advised against trying to repair a troubled marriage with "just a walk," he encouraged his readers with statistical evidence of the benefits couples derive from walking.

Dick and I talked about the article and left it on the coffee table where Jane, then sixteen, picked it up and read it. "I don't get it," she said. "Why's walking such a big deal?" It took a while, but she did get her answer.

When Dick and I first began walking through the neighborhood, our motives were simple: We needed exercise, and Jenny, our big yellow Lab, needed a nightly workout. However, as our four children became teenagers, our reasons changed.

We needed space and time alone, counting on the walk as a precious forty-five-minute respite from answering

Carol Greenwood

homework questions and negotiating TV time. Then, gradually—almost imperceptibly—we felt the benefits accumulate.

We discovered we could sort through a disagreement or
wrestle with a financial decision as we padded through the
neighborhood. We could rhapsodize about the neighbors'
flowers or their Christmas decorations. Or we didn't have to
talk at all. We could just watch the sun sink behind the Olym-
pic Mountains or let the winter rain drizzle across our faces.
By the time we returned, the dog would be too tired to bark
at the moon, but we'd be rejuvenated—physically by the exercise, emotionally and spiritually by just walking quietly
together.

Sometimes, for a change of scenery, we enjoyed walking
the three miles around Seattle's Green Lake. One Saturday,
daughter Gail joined us as we headed out before dusk. A
former newspaper reporter, Gail thrives on adventure. As
usual, she had a proposal: "Let's keep track of all the walkers
we pass and compare notes over a Coke on the way home."
So, reversing direction, we faced the walkers head-on, intent
on tallying the great diversity of the human race in fifty minutes.

Imagination in full gear, I started silently counting: Two
sisters giggling about last night's slumber party. A hand-hold-
ing middle-aged couple. A thirty-year-old pushing his
disabled father in a wheelchair. Two turbaned men chatting
amicably. A family of four—mom, dad, a baby in a backpack
and a toddler in a stroller. A bearded man with a walking
stick. Two joggers steaming by in their sweat suits and
headbands. A couple of career women analyzing their office
personnel problems. And on and on until Coke time.

Our impressions were different, yet as we tossed them
around the table in the deli they were strikingly similar.

"It seems like more happens than just conversation when
people walk together. There's closeness and intimacy."

"I sensed real communication—and a lot of listening."

"Almost everyone walked in step."

"Even those who walked by themselves didn't seem alone in the community of fellow walkers."

"Some couldn't have made it alone."

"Neither can we," Dick interjected. That was it! The clincher, the "big deal" about walking.

We were never meant to walk alone. Ever. Not on this earth. From the beginning God reached out to walk with Adam, with Noah and with His friend Abraham. All the while He kept telling His people, *I will walk among you and be your God, and you will be my people* (Leviticus 26:12).

Commitment. God didn't draw back because of floods or giants or fiery furnaces or wars or scary places like the valley of the shadow. His promises never wavered, even when His people chose to walk with other gods, when they found it too hard to walk with a God they couldn't see. When His promises and miracles weren't enough for them.

Finally, God came and walked with us in person. He came to a dusty hick town, not in kingly robes, but in the vulnerability of a helpless infant to begin His mission of getting us to our Father. Theologians call it the "incarnation," that wonderful miracle of God's coming to us in human form, to walk with us, to love, rescue and forgive us, to share His heart along the way, even to the point of the cross.

And that's a "big deal." Walking with Jesus is, in fact, the biggest deal there is. No wonder the angels pulled out all the stops and announced His birth in heavenly song. They must have known we cannot make it walking alone and that Help had finally come.

Christmas Music

*N*either my husband nor I qualify as opera buffs. In fact, between us, we haven't a trace of a musical gene. But a few years ago, we took a chance and spent a Sunday afternoon at the opera where, in spite of our musical ignorance, we got hooked.

We couldn't believe it ourselves. When the arias and the choruses exploded with romantic ecstasy on one hand or soul-wrenching agony on the other, the distance between us and the actors evaporated. Their joy or pain became ours. It was heart-to-heart stuff, like an emotional aerobic workout set to classical music. Even as novices, we knew we wanted more.

So when *Madame Butterfly* came to town, Dick and I went. In our naivete, we never realized this opera was one of the emotional "biggies," although we should have suspected it when several friends warned us to take handkerchiefs.

We should have had a clue when we read the director's words in the program: "Everyone relates to betrayal… ." Even so, no warning could have prepared us for the final scene.

Butterfly, a Japanese geisha, has waited three long years for her American naval-lieutenant husband to come back to her "when the robins nest again," as he promised. Her confidence in his return is unswerving, although others see that for Pinkerton the marriage was only a passionate fling, a "sham marriage." Gently, they try to persuade her to give up believing he'll return.

Her faith in Pinkerton, however, is unshakable, and she tells us so in the incredibly beautiful aria, "Some Day He'll Come."

Finally, his ship sails into the harbor. Pinkerton has returned to Japan. But he's not come for Butterfly, and he's not come alone. He's brought his American bride with him—to take his and Butterfly's little son back with them.

Betrayal. The sting of it flies tangibly to the audience. Butterfly gave her heart to Pinkerton. In return, he betrayed her. Devastated. Distraught. With nothing now to live for, she takes her life.

Silence. Stunned silence. Betrayal's impact swept over the audience in one crushing wave. I reached for my handkerchief. Dick reached for his. All around us in the big Seattle Opera house, people were sniffling and blowing. The woman next to me doubled over in full-blown sobs.

A red-eyed crowd stood for the curtain call, clapping wildly. Butterfly swept low in her final bow, and the audience, from the main floor to the second balcony, threw off all restraints and let go: "Bravo, bravo, bravo!" These weren't just the shouts of music critics or opera buffs enraptured with an outstanding soprano voice. These were cries from people whose hearts ached for Butterfly. They identified with the pain of her rejection.

Then came Pinkerton's turn. No one could deny the tenor's powerful voice and skillful acting. But objectivity faded fast in that charged atmosphere. To divorce his performance from his role as betrayer was too difficult. Not only did the applause lessen, but a few unbridled boo's shot out from the audience.

A Rose for Nana

Like the program said, "Everyone relates to betrayal." We experience it even before we learn the word. Our parents sneak out the back door, leaving us with a babysitter, and our little hearts scream in terror. The next time that babysitter comes, our guard is up. The first brick of a self-protective wall falls into place.

The girlfriend who promised to keep our deepest secret, doesn't, and it gets back to us. We overhear teachers laugh in the lunchroom about our "stupid" answer in class. Our parents get a divorce. The betrayal syndrome cranks into motion: Brick by brick, the wall grows higher.

If left unchecked, the progression is insidious. By adulthood, when we think the world should finally quit handing us betrayal on a silver platter, we find instead we're in the "big time." Our precious kids turn on us and call us failures; our bosses give the promotion to someone else; the church hurts us; then, to some, the worst of all pain—our spouse leaves us for someone else.

No wonder people in the opera house cried—and booed. Show us betrayal, and we relate. We want to rescue poor Butterfly, kill the villain and commend ourselves for staying inside our own little protective walls where we feel safe. We want to do anything but admit that the real culprit is not the villain outside us, but our own choice to hold back our heart from the One who made it. Instead of getting free, we set ourselves up for more betrayal.

"Some Day He'll Come." Butterfly's song reminds us of the Old Testament prophets' message, the word of hope preached to skeptical, stubborn, hurting hearts: Someday the Messiah, a savior/lover, will come.

The incredible Christmas news is that Jesus will never betray us. He is no Pinkerton. He will rescue us with His unfailing love, take our hearts in His hands and fill them to overflowing.

Carol Greenwood

This Christmas, give Jesus your heart—again. And again. And again. Then listen carefully. You'll hear the sound of bricks falling from your wall of self-protection. And that's Christmas music!

The Gift That Lasts

I still remember my favorite Christmas gift, Nancy Anne, a doll with real hair. She arrived under the Christmas tree wearing a green sweater hand knit by my Danish grandmother, a green taffeta dress and white buckle shoes.

Marvel upon marvels, Nancy Anne's bright eyes blinked open and shut when I moved her head. (This was long before battery implants enabled dolls to walk and talk to their young mothers.) Her silky, soft red hair was incredibly pliable and invited my seven-year-old fingers to braid and curl it for hours at a time, despite the adults' warning that it wouldn't last if I continued to do so.

The adults, it turned out, were right. Nancy Anne's hair didn't last very long, and neither did she. Literally loved to pieces, she eventually was replaced by other dolls.

This side of Heaven, it seems, our gifts don't last forever. Even those that delight us the most have a limited life span, and their ability to affect our lives is, at best, temporary.

Each Christmas, however, I recall another gift, one which will forever impact my life. Because of this gift, my "head" knowledge of the Gospel was pushed a lot closer to "heart" knowledge, of actually *believing* that the Gospel really is God's Good News to this world.

My remarkable gift was a young woman named Dixie. She was, I'm certain, God-sent. Who else but God could have orchestrated such incredible, extravagant love by frustrating the hopelessness of a terminal illness, and, at the same time, use Dixie to make a timid Christian bold in proclaiming the Gospel? Who else could have graphically illustrated the power of forgiveness to transform a life?

Dixie was an out-of-town cancer patient needing local visitors to fill in for distant friends and family. My intentions were noble enough, but I was woefully ignorant of how to communicate with a dying person, let alone share the love of Jesus on a personal basis.

By the time I met Dixie, she weighed about ninety-five pounds; the disease had advanced rapidly, and her physical vitality was nearly depleted. Yet her mind was razor-sharp. I can still hear her gravelly voice verbally pinning me to the hospital wall as she tried to get her do-good visitor to answer her questions about God.

"How come you're bothering with me? You've probably got a lot of better things to do than waste your time visiting a cancer patient you don't even know. What happened—did your church run out of things to do and needed another project?"

Dixie's rapid-fire barrage caught me up short. I was disarmed. She was a *person*, not a *project*, and after her initial monologue I never forgot that distinction.

"Well, I *am* from a church," I managed. "And I'd just like to spend some time with you since you're so far from your home."

"From a church, huh? So what do you have to offer? I could use some good news about now."

Startled by her abruptness, I plunged ahead. "We like to reach out, to help people." But as I looked at Dixie, little more than skin and bones, her dark eyes disclosing her hopelessness, my words suddenly sounded trite and hollow. "We try our best to give people a hand, like take over a casserole or babysit in emergencies. It's part of the Gospel, you know, to show God's love... ."

As weak as she was, Dixie pulled herself up in bed, leaned on one elbow and challenged me. "I obviously don't need a casserole or a babysitter. What I need to know is whether or not God will forgive this old milltown prostitute and show up and love me before I die. And don't give me a part of the Gospel; either it's all good news or it's nothing."

She lay back on her pillow, only to add her final zinger: "Unless you've got the guts to tell it straight, don't waste your time."

I struggled all night with what she said. I had never learned to evangelize. But Dixie didn't have time to wait for me to learn how—she needed the Gospel now.

The next morning I strode resolutely into Room 203. Dixie lay curled in a fetal position, breathing heavily. I took hold of her thin hand and spelled out the Gospel like I'd never done before: "Jesus loves you, Dixie. He died to save you from your sins. He wants you to receive His gift of life."

A few questions later and, miracle of miracles, Dixie opened her eyes and looked at me. In a voice hoarse from pain killers, she whispered, "That's good news. I believe it."

The Gospel took root, and, in Dixie's remaining days, I saw a spiritual revolution. From bitterness to peace. From guilt to forgiveness. From anger to joy. From death to life.

God's gift to Dixie was eternal salvation. His gift to me was Dixie. From her I learned what Paul meant when he wrote, *"I am not ashamed of the gospel, because it is the power of God for the salvation of everyone who believes"* (Romans 1:16).

Now that's a Christmas gift that lasts.

CHAPTER TWELVE

A

Touch

at

Easter

"I know that my Redeemer lives."

Job 19:25

The Center of the World

My brother and I once tried to find the center of the world. We were out in the back pasture on our grandparents' chicken farm, idly excavating a fort when we hit upon the idea of doing some big-time digging. An exhilarating idea. We were positive we could reach the core of the earth, probably before noon, if we worked hard.

That would mean digging *straight*. But, we didn't want to go too far and end up in China, awash in the Yangtze River, struggling to climb aboard a rescuing junk. And unable to understand Chinese, how could we communicate our plight or explain our dietary necessities, especially that we preferred peanut butter and jelly sandwiches with milk to rice and tea?

We started in, armed with one hand trowel, one garden claw and unlimited optimism about our "dig." Pitching the dirt recklessly behind us, we let our imaginations soar.

"Maybe we'll strike oil or gold or hit a little silver lode." My brother was two grades ahead of me and a lot more knowledgeable about the innards of the earth—and the buying power of the dollar. Our potential millionaire status was already flowing in his blood. "I even know the pages in the Sears catalog where I could order a new fishing pole and a new bike," he said.

I caught on quickly. "My bike is the only one at school with skinny tires. I *need* a new one. And a new jacket. Nobody else has one with big, baggy sleeves like mine. I hate it."

The possibilities were limitless. The more we thought about them, the faster we dug. Even Rex, our cocker spaniel, caught our exploratory bug and peered into the growing cavity, giving an occasional dig himself and rubbing his dirt-caked nose against our eager faces.

Unfortunately, the dark side of human nature soon reared its ugly head. I can't remember why. I may have given one too many suggestions to speed up the project or advocated changing tools. Whatever the antagonism, war broke out, and as the youngest, I got the brunt of it. Dirt balls flew. I caught it in the back and head. I flew to the house screaming and tattling: "David's trying to kill me."

So it was that our ambitious venture stalemated with a lunch break and a half-dug hole. We later had to backfill that hole so that the renter's cows wouldn't fall in and break their legs. But alas, we never reached the center of the world, and our scientific zeal died a quiet death along with our hopes of new bikes, fishing poles and jackets as we munched our way through a peanut butter sandwich and back to reality.

Years ago, when our first granddaughter, Andrea, was nearly two years old, she had a clear understanding of the center of the world. Not only did she know its location, she also knew how to get there—just by being herself.

It's not too hard to figure out when you're the first child and the first grandchild: *The world revolves around me.* Adults jump at the opportunity to run and fetch when your needs demand attention. Cameras flash when you do something extraordinarily cute, and pens record your clever early words.

Indeed, not only is the world your oyster, but the center of it is *you*.

Andrea captivated our whole family as her little tow-headed body bounced through our lives. Inquisitiveness in high gear. A knockout smile that melted your heart in seconds.

However—like all the other grandchildren who have followed—as she approached two, we saw signs of change. Innocence began to wear a different hat—like an occasional foot stomping when a second cookie is denied, a loud wail to protest bedtime or resist being belted into her car seat. Yes, for each child the discovery comes as a bit of a shock: *The world does not revolve around me!* And we are all foolish to think that we can live happily believing that it does. The Bible makes that pretty clear.

Where is the center of the world? Our orchardist friend, John, challenged me on that issue a week before a plane crash took his life. Patient, laid-back, a man of few words, John had an instinct for good timing and a gift for quietly delivering "zingers."

He stood next to me washing apples at our annual cider weekend on his forty-acre apple ranch in Eastern Washington. With fifteen people talking and scrubbing apples, the conversation runs the gamut of crops, weather, sports, kids and politics. No one is shy in this group. In fact, talk comes before work, except for John, who mostly listened.

Oblivious to my single-tracked contribution, I talked about the concerts *in Seattle*, the football games *in Seattle*, the opera *in Seattle*, the flowers *in Seattle*, etc., etc., ad nauseam *in Seattle*.

Finally, John had had enough. Leaning over in front of my face, apple in hand like a miniature globe, he spoke one simple but profound sentence. "Carol, " he said. "Seattle is not the center of the world." I reeled, but I heard him. This was more than our good-natured cross-state, rural/urban bantering. This was truth battering my self-centered little world. Wonderful truth, freeing truth.

Where is the center of the world? The Easter story has the answer. Jesus' death and resurrection offers us the only hope for living outside of our selfish worlds with our tight self-defined boundaries and petty agendas. For we see, in Christ, God's provision: Someone bought us with a price. And more. Someone freed us from believing and living like life is about us. Someone opened up a whole new world where our center could be turned and life could be lived out of abundance, not scarcity. We could not only be recipients of God's grace, we could pass it along to others.

Where's the center of the world? Of the universe? If you have questions, friends, check in at the cross of Christ.

Man on the Loose

We were all freezing. Ten of us in our adult class. We shivered together and blew icy puffs into the frosty air of our church fireside room. After a week of sixty-degree days, we weren't prepared for the thirty-degree temperature drop. Nor was the janitor who'd neglected to turn up the heat.

March can be a topsy-turvy, yo-yo month in the Pacific Northwest. Spring saunters in unannounced, and then just as we shelve our scarves and gloves, winter barges back in, determined to clutch us a little longer.

This particular morning, however, we were rescued from complaining about the weather by the sounds of coffee perking on the sideboard and logs crackling in the fireplace. Our disappointment assuaged by the prospects of immediate human comforts, we settled in for our assault on Romans 6.

Then, just as we started grappling with Paul's explanation of law and grace, the door swung open and in stormed a dirty, disheveled young man. Dressed in heavy trousers and layers of ragged sweaters topped with a rumpled overcoat, he marched past our table and plunked down on the sofa facing the fireplace.

He cleared his throat. We turned and stared. He rubbed his red hands. We looked at each other wondering: *Who is this guy?*

He plopped two logs on the fire and headed for the coffee. We swiveled in our chairs, following his actions. My husband, leader of the study, finally broke the silence. "Would you like a cup of coffee?"

"Yup."

"You're welcome to pull up a chair and join our Bible class," Dick offered.

Another one-word answer: "Nope."

I remembered the food left over from our packing boxes for the food bank and knew we could make him breakfast on the spot. "How about some toast and fruit juice to go with your coffee?"

"No." His answer was pointed. No more offers.

We resumed our class. I felt uneasy, however, with our stranger-guest, and so I watched him out of the corner of my eye. He didn't stay seated long, but popped up and strolled over to the piano where he played a couple of scales. Then, bowing to his imaginary audience, he returned to the fireplace, positioned himself cross-legged in front of it and began blowing on the fire.

I had difficulty concentrating on Romans 6. Questions cascaded through my mind: *Can we help this guy? Why are his eyes so wild-looking? Is he on drugs? Perhaps mentally ill? Should we usher him out?*

Ambivalent feelings. I had a good case of them. Someone had stumbled into the Lord's house on His day, and here we were reading His Word, torn between compassion and fear, wanting to reach out, but scared of this wild man.

As we were winding up the class, our stranger-friend abruptly left the room and headed toward the sanctuary where the eleven-o'clock service was about to begin. When we entered the sanctuary, I saw him write a note and place it on the lectern. Apparently satisfied his note would be read, he sat in the front pew, only to hop up and play another scale on the sanctuary piano.

By this time the congregation was aware of the stranger's presence. Whispering was rampant. A couple of people, uneasy with the smell and unpredictable behavior of the man, moved across the aisle. Ushers were poised to pounce if necessary, yet they seemed nervous and uncertain about what they would do. Our pastor gave the announcements, but he ignored the note—a demand, we learned later, for a million dollars.

Finally, in the middle of the sermon, our unknown visitor stood to his feet and strode down the side aisle and outside to the chilly March morning. Gone from our midst.

We talked about it after church. Could we have helped him? Should we have called the police or the drug rehab center down the street? The consensus was that we'd better think of some strategies for next time. After all, what would we do if a mad man *really* got loose in our church? Imagine!

Then I remembered another Man on the loose, a Man in first-century Palestine. He wasn't mad or even potentially dangerous like our Sunday morning stranger may have been, although some claimed He was. He, too, burst upon the scene, upset the status quo and did what no one before had ever done, especially in "religious" circles. Wild, unpredictable, scandalous things.

Outrageous things. Things like forgiving undeserving people and accepting sinners even before they repented. Things like welcoming home dirty, wayward kids or healing people with tainted pasts. Things like talking to women as equals and eating supper with cheaters. Extravagant things like loving us as we are instead of as we ought to be. And finally, dying to pay the price of all our rebellion.

But the Easter news tells us that this Someone still lives. Jesus, God's Man, lives! Oh, what would happen if we dared loose Him—in our private worlds, our homes, our churches?

Closing the Gap

"Hey, Lady, you gonna go to heaven?" The question shot out of nowhere, and I ignored it. But like radar tracking, it honed in on its target. "Yeah, *you*, lady." No doubt about it, the young man leaning against the airport concourse wall was questioning me.

I slipped my carry-on bag and purse onto the conveyor belt of the metal detector and called back my answer: "You bet I'm going to Heaven." End of conversation and on to the boarding gate where those headed for a conference in New Orleans were talking animatedly. In all the excitement, no one mentioned being questioned by the twentyish-looking guy who'd apparently quizzed others about their eternal destiny.

However, later, as I walked down the jetway, I overheard the passengers behind me laughing about a "religious nut" who'd polled them about their ticket to Heaven. I smiled smugly as I handed my ticket to the flight attendant, mentally replaying the earlier query as I stepped aboard: *Hey, lady, you gonna go to Heaven?* I basked in my confident answer, my awareness of my salvation in Christ. It felt good to know that the fear of death did not grip me.

Fearful? Not me. Nevertheless, I found myself paying close attention to the preflight emergency instructions. I turned my head to check the location of the nearest emergency exit. I even admitted to myself that I liked the overtones of competence and experience in the captain's voice when he introduced himself and sketched our route. Aloft, I relaxed, settling in for the ride to New Orleans, alternately reading *James Herriott's Dog Stories* and dozing as the plane headed south. This, indeed, was smooth sailing.

Smooth, that is, until an unexpected bounce jolted me awake. The seat belt sign lit up, and simultaneously the captain reassured us: "We're experiencing a little turbulence. If it doesn't smooth out, we'll find a higher altitude. Meanwhile, relax and keep your seat belts fastened."

The plane bounced along like a jeep over a washboard road. I didn't like it at all, but I diverted myself by leaning forward to peer out the window at the snow-capped Rockies below. I cinched in my seatbelt, and as I did, my book slid off my lap to the floor. Bending over to retrieve it, I noticed my hands were wet and sticky—in a word, clammy.

You gonna go to Heaven, lady? The words echoed again, but this time my smugness was dissipating. My clammy hands were more honest than my thoughts. *Okay, Lord,* I admitted, *I know I'm going to Heaven. I'd just prefer not to go today.*

Safe landings have a way of restoring perspective and objectivity, of allowing us another opportunity to view the gaps between what we believe in our heads and what our hearts tell us. "Carol," I said later when I faced myself in the mirror, "you may be certain of Heaven, but you're scared about getting there too soon. Where's your faith?"

The eighteen-inch gap between my head and my heart grabbed my attention. Familiar territory for this pilgrim. Others, I'm sure, have battled that same gap, that chasm separating what we want to believe and what our hearts actually tell us. Who of us has not grappled with it and come up gasping for help as reality poked holes in our pious pretensions?

Despite its many faces, "the gap" is easily recognizable. Like late-night TV reruns, the scenarios we experience are incredibly common. We're overlooked for a shower invitation and our head knows why—too many relatives to include—but our heart, because it has absorbed hurts and negative messages in the past, gives us another story: They didn't want us. We think we believe that God loves us unconditionally. Yet, when we lose our temper at our kids, our heart condemns us with the indictment that we've now blown it—we've stepped over the line of God's grace and become unlovable.

How often I've bemoaned that gap. How often most of us have faced that distance between head knowledge and heart belief and felt we were looking across the Grand Canyon. Surely we ought to be more spiritually advanced than this! Why do we "lose it" so easily? Why do our wounded hearts continue to play havoc with our faith? And why do we then proceed to spiral down from exasperation to self-condemnation? What will ever close this gap?

The Lord never seems to take on my questions as a celestial high priority. Jesus, it seems, doesn't traffic in *why*'s and *whatever*'s. Remember how He dismissed the disciples' question about the man born blind? Assigning blame or analyzing faults wasn't Jesus' mission. He came to bring glory to His Father. He did it then and He continues to do it now—heal the sick and restore broken, wounded hearts. And to exchange our fears for faith in His Father's provision for our lives.

Again, I'm brought up short by Jesus and the good news of His death and resurrection. His offer of twenty-four-hour service with a prepaid price. It's the "Easter special" once more, where the empty tomb overrides our clammy-hand syndrome, and the grace of the victorious Christ reaches out to close that cavernous gap between our heads and our hearts.

Hey, lady, you gonna go to Heaven?

You bet. And I'm going first-class. My ticket's stamped with the cross.

Outrageous Faith

"here in the world did we get four bags of dried-up onions?" my husband asked as he walked through the utility room. "Unless you're planning to make onion soup for the whole neighborhood, I say, 'Let's toss these out.'"

"If you don't, I will," chimed in daughter Jane. "Those dead things have been sitting around here for a month. Even the dog won't chew them."

That was in the fall, and I wasn't about to divulge the contents of the mystery bags then nor did I want the "onions" thrown out. So I silenced them with the promise I'd take care of the matter myself. I knew that five months later the secret would be out, not only for Dick and Jane, but also for our whole neighborhood and anyone else who passed by our street. Our house would be surrounded by the brightest yellow spectacle imaginable—one hundred giant Holland daffodils blooming their hybrid hearts out.

Through all the dark days of winter, I silently relished the moment when the first signs of my surprise would surface, when someone would spot the fresh green foliage pressing through the waterlogged soil and demand to know what was happening in our hitherto barren flower beds. And even when I occasionally forgot about my secret "underground" project, another healthy rainstorm would remind me of that dreary October afternoon when a spunky, redheaded nursery clerk challenged me to fight an attack of doubt with a visible statement of faith.

Torrential rains fell that day as I drove home from work. The racing windshield wipers barely cleared the windshield fast enough, and, even with headlights on, visibility was near zero. Inching along in the three-o'clock traffic, I longed to be home by my fireplace, listening to good music and enjoying a cup of tea.

I wasn't just battling the elements outside: I was also fighting a grief attack inside. Between the dreary weather and the pain of losing a close friend, my faith was at a low ebb. In fact, it crossed my mind that perhaps it was on a day like this that Job asked, "If a man dies, will he live again?"

I remembered that the sky was dark when Jesus cried out from the cross, "My God, My God, why have You forsaken Me?"

I wondered what the day was like after the crucifixion when Peter, discouraged at the loss of his beloved master, said, "I'm going fishing."

Right in the middle of these thoughts, my eye caught a big red sign, barely visible through the rainstorm: "Sale—Giant Holland Bulbs—Plant Now."

Crazy. Foolish. Wild. But I did it anyway. I braked, made a quick left turn into the parking lot of the nursery, leapt from the car and dashed through the downpour.

"A customer! I can't believe anyone would even get out of a car today," sang out the cheery, red-haired clerk. "This weather isn't fit for man or beast. The only thing that could bring anyone in today is either insanity or some kind of outrageous faith."

"I want one hundred Holland daffodil bulbs," I said.

206

"One hundred daffodils. Indeed, a woman of faith on a day like this." The clerk was ecstatic. She scooped up a handful of bulbs from the adjacent bin, plucking out a large one to hold up between us.

"Now I'd call this a miracle in the making. Look at this scruffy thing—hardly more than a dried-up onion on its last legs. But, if you plant it six inches deep in loose soil, with a scattering of fertilizer and, if you're willing to wait five months, you're in for a burst of blinding color just when you've given up hope. With one hundred of these bulbs, my dear, your garden's going to be singing 'Alleluia' next spring."

Had she somehow been privy to my thoughts of the last few hours? Or was she an angel in disguise? It didn't matter. Her words rang true, and they bulldozed my doubts.

I quietly gathered up the four big bags and headed home, eager for the first dry day to plant the bulbs. I was ready to make my statement of faith.

If a man dies, will he live again? "Yes!" shout the Scriptures. Jesus' resurrection is historical fact. God's Son died and lives again. If we don't believe this, says Paul, we are foolish and to be greatly pitied.

Will our God ever forsake us? "No!" shout the Scriptures again. Jesus' death and resurrection has sealed our relationship with the Father and guaranteed our life with Him forever.

Do we dare give up and just "go fishing" like Peter, during those dark days when we see no hope? No! Remember the resurrection of our Lord!

This Easter we'll be celebrating His resurrection with the help of one hundred blooming daffodils. And we'll be singing "Alleluia." God has conquered death!

The red-haired clerk would call it "outrageous faith."